A WHOLLY HEALTHY GLASGOW

IAIN HEGGIE

The Royal Court Writers Series
published by Methuen
in association with the Royal Court Theatre

ROYAL COURT WRITERS SERIES

First published in 1988 as a Methuen paperback original in Great Britain by
Methuen London Ltd, 11 New Fetter Lane, London EC4P 4EE
and in the United States of America
by Methuen Inc, 29 West 35th Street, New York, NY 10001
in association with the Royal Court Theatre, Sloane Square, London SW1

Printed in Great Britain by Expression Printers Ltd, London N7

CAUTION
All rights whatsoever in this play are strictly reserved and application for performance etc,
should be made before rehearsals begin to A. P. Watt Ltd, of 20 John Street, London
WC1N 2DL. No performance may be given unless a licence has been obtained.

THE NEW PATRONAGE SCHEME AT THE ROYAL COURT

For the last three years the Royal Court has had to supplement its box office earnings and government grants with fund-raising from private business sources. While we have been relatively successful in meeting our fundraising targets and recent years have seen better and better earnings from the box office, the future looks as difficult as ever, in spite of the Arts Minister's announcement of a three-year increase in the Arts Council's grant-in-aid.

Increasingly, therefore, the Royal Court needs a body of regular support in its fundraising drive and so we are introducing our new patronage scheme. For many years now Members of the Royal Court Theatre Society have received special notice of new productions and priority booking, but why not consider contributing £35 (or £50 joint membership) and become a **Friend of the Royal Court** — or approach your company or business to become an **Associate** or a **Patron**, thereby involving yourself directly in maintaining the high standard and unique quality of Royal Court productions — while enjoying complimentary tickets to the shows themselves?

1 MEMBERSHIP SCHEME

For £10 you will receive details of all forthcoming events via the Royal Court *Member's Letter*; be given priority booking at the box office and be entitled to purchase any available seat for £3 during previews (maximum of two per Member).

2 FRIENDS OF THE ROYAL COURT

For £35 (or £50 joint membership) you will be entitled to one (or two) complimentary preview ticket(s) for performances on the Main Stage and one (or two) exchange vouchers for productions in the Theatre Upstairs. You will automatically be on our mailing list and be invited to all lectures and special events.

3 ASSOCIATES OF THE ROYAL COURT

For £350 you will be entitled to two top priority tickets (previews or press nights) to all Main House productions, two tickets to all plays in the Theatre Upstairs and priority block ticket-booking availability. You will also be invited to a special Associates lunch on stage and also the Annual Associates Cocktail Party/Lecture. If desired, you can appear in the Royal Court programme and be presented with a certificate stating your membership of this exclusive club.

4 INDIVIDUAL PATRONS

For £1,000 you can make a 'personal appearance' on a plaque in the Royal Court lobby, appear in our programme and be invited to a special glittering event. In addition, you will be entitled to ten free tickets for five shows in the Main House or the Theatre Upstairs.

When you have chosen fro the five categories, please make your cheque/P.O. payable to the *Royal Court Theatre Society* and send to: *Max Stafford-Clark, Artistic Director, Royal Court Theatre, Sloane Square, London SW1*. Alternatively, if you wish to covenant for four years or more by filling in the form which you will find in the theatre foyer, we — as a registered charity — can claim back the tax you have already paid, thereby increasing the value of your donation.

COMING NEXT

IN THE MAIN HOUSE 730 1745

From 3 March

The Royal Court Theatre, The Leicester Haymarket and The Wrestling School present

THE LAST SUPPER

By Howard Barker. Directed by Kenny Ireland

A play about failing charisma. Lvov, a messianic figure, sensing the deterioration of his powers, summons his 12 followers to a farewell dinner and presents to them 8 parables that summarise his teachings and which reveal a model of social behaviour as extraordinary as the model provided by Christ.

IN THE THEATRE UPSTAIRS 730 2554

From 11 February

The Women's Playhouse Trust in association with the Royal Court Theatre presents

LOW LEVEL PANIC

By Clare McIntyre. Directed by Nancy Meckler

"If you look really sexy you might get assaulted. You might get assaulted anyway. In your fantasies, looking very sexy, you dice with danger In reality you might not want that at all.
The play is set in a bathroom and has no axe to grind." Clare McIntyre

From January - April 1988

A high proportion of the plays we have produced on our two stages over the years are plays we have commissioned. But two of the outstanding successes at the Royal Court in '87 — THE EMPEROR and SERIOUS MONEY — started in workshops with actors, a playwright and a director. SERIOUS MONEY began with Max Stafford-Clark, Caryl Churchill and an acting company investigating the mysteries of the City before Caryl started to write the play. Likewise with THE EMPEROR, Michael Hastings and Jonathan Miller were both keen to stage a version of Kapuscinski's book, and they experimented with a group of actors, to find a theatrical form for the text before committing to a full production.

We are keen to 'kickstart' more work in this way — obviously in conjuction with our existing policy of commissions to playwrights of all levels of experience.

We have no studio or laboratory space at the Royal Court Theatre, so early in '88 the Theatre Upstairs will be closed to allow an extensive period of development to take place. Our purpose will not only be to find new plays but also to investigate new areas and forms of work.

Readings and presentations of some of the resulting work will be open to the public. Details will be advertised.

AND AT WYNDHAM'S THEATRE

SERIOUS MONEY

By Caryl Churchill. Directed by Max Stafford-Clark

Box Office 836 3028   CC 379 6565/4444 (Open all hours)   741 9999   Groups 836 3962
"*Love the City or Hate it, but see this*" DAILY TELEGRAPH

ROYAL COURT EXTRAS

ST. VALENTINE'S PARTY

The Royal Court Theatre is in its 100th Anniversary Year! Celebrate at a ST. VALENTINE'S PARTY at CAFE MAXIMS, Panton Street, London SW1. Saturday 13th February. Tickets £35 each. Telephone Anne-Marie Thompson on 01 373 4674

IAIN HEGGIE CURTAINRAISER

THE CAKE and
WAITING FOR SHUGGIE'S MA

Two short plays by Iain Heggie. Directed by Lindsay Posner.

Wednesday 10 February at 6pm in the Main House

A Wholly Healthy Glasgow

BY IAIN HEGGIE

A winner in the 1985 Mobil Playwriting Competition

DONALD DICK, Masseur .... TOM WATSON
CHARLEY HOOD, Senior Instructor .... GERARD KELLY
MURDO CALDWELL, Junior Instructor .... PAUL HIGGINS

Director .... Richard Wilson
Designer .... Sue Plummer
Lighting Designer .... Paul Pyant
Sound Designer .... Ros Elliman

THERE WILL BE ONE INTERVAL OF 15 MINUTES

The first performance of *A Wholly Healthy Glasgow* was at
The Royal Exchange Theatre, Manchester on 29 January 1987

FOR THIS PRODUCTION

Company Stage Manager .... Ann Harrison Baxter
Deputy Stage Manager .... Patrick Watkinson
Assistant Stage Manager .... Kim Ford
Production Manager .... Paul R. Griffin
Production Photographs .... Kevin Cummings
Poster Design .... Angus

FOR THE ROYAL EXCHANGE THEATRE COMPANY

Artistic Directors .... Gregory Hersov, James Maxwell, Braham Murray, Caspar Wrede
Associate Artistic Directors .... Nicholas Hytner, Ian McDiarmid, Sophie Marshall
Administrator .... Lynda Farran
Production Manager .... James Williams
Staff Contracts & Special Projects Manager .... Denise Wood
Financial Controller .... David Fairclough
Press & Publicity Director .... David Fraser (061-833 0038)

The Royal Court Theatre is financially assisted by The Arts Council of Great Britain, the Royal Borough of Kensington and Chelsea and the London Borough Grants Scheme.

The Royal Exchange Theatre is Financially Assisted by the Arts Council of Great Britain and by the ten Districts of Greater Manchester.

Arts Council Funded

THE ROYAL EXCHANGE THEATRE COMPANY

The Royal Exchange Theatre Company was formed in 1976 by a group of directors whose association had begun 17 years previously with the 59 Theatre Company at the Lyric Hammersmith and continued with the Manchester-based 69 Theatre Company. Recognised nationally and internationally as one of the country's leading theatre companies, the Royal Exchange has had 17 of its productions transfer to London, made several national tours in its specially constructed mobile theatre, and toured to seven European countries. Its reputation has attracted stars like Albert Finney, Tom Courtenay, Edward Fox, Vanessa Redgrave, Ben Kingsley, Helen Mirren, Leo McKern, Paul Schofield, Julie Walters, Michael Hordern and Robert Lindsay.

The Royal Exchange — the company's home — is one of the most unusual theatres in the world — a striking glass and steel structure, often likened to a spaceship in appearance, which sits in the grandeur of a huge Edwardian hall, Manchester's former Cotton Exchange. It is a unique theatre-in-the-round built with the express purpose of freeing the imagination of the dramatist, actor and audience. It seats 740 people within 30 feet of the performance space, giving the auditorium an extraordinary intimacy.

The architectural marriage of old and new is mirrored in the choice of repertoire and style of production. The Company has staged classics from all periods, many new plays (including several from the Mobil Playwriting Competition) and musicals, European and British premieres. One play created for the Royal Exchange — Ronald Harwood's *The Dresser* — has been seen all over the world on stage and screen. Another Royal Exchange commission, the award-winning *Masterpieces* by Sarah Daniels, was subsequently seen at the Royal Court.

TOM WATSON (Donald Dick) was born in Auchinleck, Ayrshire and has enjoyed great success both on television and in theatre. His many television appearances have included leading roles in *Weire of Hermiston*, *The Canterbury Tales* (The Miller), *Treasure Island* (Israel Hands), *The Slab Boys*, *The Campbells* and *Taggart*. Appearances for Granada have included *Village Hall* and *Ghosts of Motley Hall*. Recently he has worked for Yorkshire TV on *Dreams Lost, Dreams Found* and for BBC Radio Scotland on *City Lights* and *A Wholly Healthy Glasgow*. Extensive radio work includes currently playing Mr. Holliday in the popular Radio 4 series *King Street Junior*. Film credits: *Another Time, Another Place*, *Nosey Dobson*, *Little Lord Fauntleroy* and *Haunters of the Deep*. Recent theatre work includes *The Catch* (Royal Court), *Every Good Boy Deserves a Favour* and *Bugler Boy* (Traverse, Edinburgh), *The Thrie Estaites* and *Robert Burns* (Scottish Theatre Company), *Fool for Love* (National Theatre and the Lyric Theatre), *In Time of Strife* (7.84 Company at Glasgow Citizens and Half Moon Theatre), George in *Who's Afraid of Virginia Woolf* (Brunton Theatre Musselburgh) and *The Gorbals Story* (7.84). After *A Wholly Healthy Glasgow* he takes the lead in a new BBC film directed by David Hayman, *The Govan Ghost Story*.

PAUL HIGGINS (Murdo Caldwell) was born in Wishaw and studied for five years to be a missionary priest before deciding on an acting career. His first theatre work was at Cumbernauld Theatre after which he trained at the Central School of Speech and Drama. Since leaving in 1986 he has appeared as Alistair Finn in STV's *Taggart* and at the Waterman's Arts Theatre, Brentford, the Edinburgh Festival Fringe and the Riverside Studios, in *The Lemmings are Coming* with John Gordon Sinclair. He also co-wrote *The Lemmings* and wrote and performed the music for it. He plays in the BBC film version of *A Wholly Healthy Glasgow* and has recently filmed *A Very Peculiar Practice*, and *Tumbledown*, directed by Richard Eyre, for the BBC.

GERARD KELLY (Charley Hood) has frequently appeared on television. His credits include Willie Melvin in the award winning series *City Lights*, Donal in the award-winning Play for Today *Donal and Sally*, Spanky in *The Slab Boys*, David Balfour in *Kidnapped*, Andrew Cameron in *The Camerons*, P.C. David Gallacher in *Juliet Bravo*, *The Victoria Wood Show*, and *Shoestring*, all for the BBC; *Killer* for STV and Arty Jackson in *Going Out* for Southern TV. His film credits include *Mr. Jolly Lives Next Door*, *More Bad News* and Andrew in *The Thirteenth Reunion*. Theatre credits include Spanky in *The Slab Boys Trilogy* at the Traverse Theatre, Citizens's Theatre and Royal Court Theatre, *In Time of Strife* at the Citizen's Theatre, *Man Equals Man* at the Almeida Theatre, London, and *A Wholly Healthy Glasgow* for the Royal Exchange Theatre Company in Manchester and at the Edinburgh Festival. He will soon be seen in BBC Scotland's production of *A Wholly Healthy Glasgow*.

IAIN HEGGIE (Writer) was born in Glasgow and left school at 16. After various jobs he found work in a Glasgow health club as a P.T. instructor. After moving to Birmingham to fill a similar post, he took a Humanities degree at Wolverhampton Polytechnic. Teacher training at Goldsmith's followed, and he then taught Drama in Further Education Colleges in London. He started writing full-time in 1984, and *A Wholly Healthy Glasgow* won a special prize in the Mobil playwriting competition in 1985. It was produced at the Royal Exchange Theatre Manchester in February 1987, and it was then invited to the 1987 Edinburgh Festival, where it sold out the Church Hill theatre for 2 weeks. His one-act play *Politics in the Park* was produced at the Liverpool Playhouse in 1986, and was revived at the Traverse Theatre Edinburgh in 1987. He was Arts Council Writer in Residence at the Royal Exchange 1986/7 and his new play *American Bagpipes* opens there in February 1988. Iain Heggie was a member of the Royal Court Writers' Group 1985/6, when he wrote a number of short plays including *Waiting for Shuggie's Ma* and *The Cake*, which have frequently been performed in London, Edinburgh and Manchester. He is currently working on a new play for the Royal Court, *Wilma of Scotland.*

SUE PLUMMER (Designer) studied graphic design at St. Martin's School of Art. She began working in the theatre by assisting Tim O'Brien on *The Merry Wives of Windsor* for the RSC and Peter Brook on *Oedipus* at the National Theatre. West End theatre work includes *I, Claudius* at the Queens (costumes), Michael Frayn's *Clouds* at the Duke of York, *Thee and Me* at the National Theatre and *Hamlet* at the Royal Court (costumes). Opera work includes Bizet's *The Pearl Fishers*, costumes for *Rigoletto* for the Welsh National Opera and Peter Maxwell Davies' *The Martyrdom of St. Magnus* which opened in St. Magnus Cathedral in Orkney and later transferred to the Roundhouse for the Proms. She has also designed many new plays on the London Fringe including David Edgar's *Dick Deterred* and Dusty Hughes' *Commitments* at the Bush, Dennis Potter's *Brimstone and Treacle* at the Open Space, David Halliwell's *The House* for Joint Stock, Hanif Kureishi's *Birds of Passage* and David Edgar's *That Summer* for the Hampstead Theatre, *The Overgrown Path* at the Royal Court, and *Talk of the Devil* at the Watford Palace. *A Wholly Healthy Glasgow* marked her Royal Exchange debut.

PAUL PYANT (Lighting Designer) trained at RADA in London and since 1974 has mainly been associated with *Glyndebourne Opera*. His lighting credits for opera productions include *A Midsummer Night's Dream* (Glyndebourne Festival Opera in Hong Kong), *Dream, Die Zauberflote, Orfeo, The Love for Three Oranges*, and *Simon Boccenegra* (Glyndebourne Touring Opera), *King Priam* (Kent Opera), *Orlando, The Marriage of Figaro, The Pearl Fishers* (Scottish Opera), *Figaro, The Barber of Seville* (Welsh National Opera), the award-winning *Xerxes, Carmen, Lady Macbeth of Mtsensk* (English National Opera), *Macbeth* (Opera North), and *Hansel and Gretel* (Grand Theatre, Geneva) as well as many productions for other operatic organisations including *Eugene Onegin, Les Boreades* (Royal Academy of Music), *Oberto, Faust, Die Loreley, The Devils Wall* (University College Opera), *L'Ormindo* (Guildhall School of Music) and the Brighton Festival produictions of *Peter Grimes, Boris Godanov, Queen of Spades, Andrea Chenier, The Masked Ball* for New Sussex Opera. Work away from the opera field has covered plays, musicals and ballet, including *The Lonely Road* (Old Vic), *As You Like It, The Country Wife, A Wholly Healthy Glasgow*, and *The Merchant of Venice* (Royal Exchange Theatre), and *A Place with the Pigs* (National Theatre).

RICHARD WILSON (Director) made his directorial debut at the Stables Theatre, Manchester. At the Royal Court he has directed Robert Holman's *Other Worlds, Heaven and Hell* by Dusty Hughes and *God's Second in Command* by Jacqueline Rudet. For Joint Stock he directed *The House* (David Halliwell) and *Say Your Prayers* (Nick Darke). He directed Dusty Hughes' play *Commitments* at the Bush Theatre and on Play for Today. His production of *A Wholly Healthy Glasgow* was invited to the 1987 Edinburgh Festival and he also directed it for BBC Scotland. Other BBC productions for the same slot were *The Remainder Man* by Philip Martin and *Under the Hammer* by Steven Fagan. As an actor his most recent television work was in John Byrne's *Tutti Frutti.* He will also be seen in the same writer's *Normal Service* in February and later in the year in the series *Hot Metal.* His stage work includes two Gordon Newman plays at the Royal Court — *Operation Bad Apple* and *An Honourable Trade.* Recent film work includes *A Passage to India, Whoops Apocalypse* and *Prick up your Ears.*

FOR THE ROYAL COURT

DIRECTION

Artistic Director .... MAX STAFFORD-CLARK
Deputy Director .... SIMON CURTIS
Assistant Director .... LINDSAY POSNER
Casting Director .... LISA MAKIN
Literary Manager .... KATE HARWOOD
Senior Script Associate .... MICHAEL HASTINGS*
Thames TV Writer in Residence .... HARWANT BAINS*
Secretary .... MELANIE KENYON

PRODUCTION

Production Manager... BO BARTON
Technical Manager, Theatre Upstairs........................... CHRIS BAGUST
Chief Electrician .... CHRISTOPHER TOULMIN
Deputy Chief Electrician.. MARK BRADLEY
Sound Designer .... CHRISTOPHER SHUTT
Master Carpenter.. CHRIS HARDING-ROBERTS
Deputy Carpenter.. JOHN BURGESS
Costume Supervisor .... JENNIFER COOK
Wardrobe Assistants .... IONA KENRICK, CATHIE SKILBECK

ADMINISTRATION

General Manager .... GRAHAM COWLEY
Secretary .... SAMANTHA REID
Financial Administrator .... EILEEN WENTWORTH
Financial Assistant .... GILL RUSSELL
Press & Publicity Manager .... NATASHA HARVEY
Development Director .... TOM PETZAL
Development Assistant .... JACQUELINE VIEIRA
House Manager .... GODFREY HAMILTON
Assistant House Manager.. ALISON SMITH
Bookshop Manager... DIANE PETHERICK*
Box Office Manager .... PAT GIBBONS
Box Office Assistants .... STEVEN CURRIE, GERALD BROOKING
Stage Door/Telephonists .... DIANE PETHERICK*, ANGELA TOULMIN*
Evening Stage Door .... TYRONE LUCAS*, CERI SHIELDS*
Maintenance.. JOHN LORRIGIO*
Cleaners .... EILEEN CHAPMAN*, IVY JONES*, CLIFF WOOTTON*
Firemen .... MICK BROWN*, PAUL KLEINMANN*

YOUNG PEOPLE'S THEATRE

Director .... ELYSE DODGSON
Administrator .... JANE HELLINGS
Youth Drama Worker .... SUZY GILMOUR
Schools & Comunity Liaison Worker............................. MARK HOLNESS
Writer in Residence .... KARIM ALRAWI

*Part-time staff

COUNCIL:Chairman: MATTHEW EVANS, CHRIS BAGUST, BO BARTON, STUART BURGE, ANTHONY C. BURTON, CARYL CHURCHILL, HARRIET CRUICKSHANK, SIMON CURTIS, ALLAN DAVIS, DAVID LLOYD DAVIS, ROBERT FOX, MRS. HENNY GESTETNER OBE, DEREK GRANGER, DAVID HARE, JOCELYN HERBERT, DAVID KLEEMAN, HANIF KUREISHI, SONIA MELCHETT, JOAN PLOWRIGHT CBE, GREVILLE POKE, JANE RAYNE, SIR HUGH WILLATT.

THE CAKE

a short play
by
Iain Heggie

Characters

ARCHIE   Two Glaswegian men in
DANNY   their sixties

Iain Heggie began writing short plays when he was part of the Royal Court Writers' Group in 1985-86.

The Cake was first performed as a rehearsed reading at the Royal Exchange Theatre on 14 September 1986. Directed by Michael Fox. With Ian Hastings as Archie and Martin Oldfield as Danny.

The Cake and another short play *Waiting for Shuggie's Ma*, will be given rehearsed readings as a curtainraiser to *A Wholly Healthy Glasgow* on Wednesday 10 February at 6pm. They will be directed by Lindsay Posner.

Setting
A room with a table and chairs and a telephone. On the table is a round uncut cake and a knife.

DANNY *picks up the knife and goes to cut the cake.*

ARCHIE: Don't.

DANNY: Eh?

ARCHIE: Don't cut the cake.

DANNY: Why not?

ARCHIE: Not yet!

DANNY: I was going to cut it three ways.

ARCHIE: Not till she comes.

DANNY: I was going to make three equal portions.

ARCHIE: You might embarrass her.

DANNY: Three equal portions will *save* embarrassing her.

ARCHIE: She might not want to eat a third of the cake and leave it and/

DANNY: She might be embarrassed about saying how much she'll want to eat and/

ARCHIE: And get embarrassed.

DANNY: And go hungry.

Pause. DANNY *puts down the knife.*

DANNY: I *know* your game.

ARCHIE: I'm only being considerate.

DANNY: I know your game, by the way.

ARCHIE: I'm only being considerate, by the way.

DANNY: You only want to eat more than your fair share of the cake.

ARCHIE: I was being *very* considerate when I invited her round for the cake.

DANNY: It was me that saw her, in the bakers.

ARCHIE: Aye but it was *me* that talked to her.

DANNY: It was me that found out she was lonely.

ARCHIE: It was me that *asked her round* to share the cake.

Pause.

How do you know she's lonely?

DANNY: She lives alone.

ARCHIE: She might not/

DANNY: She *said* she lives alone.

ARCHIE: She might not *be lonely*.

DANNY: And *I'm* not lonely because/

ARCHIE: Well sometimes I'm lonely and/

DANNY: Because I *don't* live alone.

ARCHIE: And I *don't* live alone.

Pause.

Do you think she'll come?

DANNY: What?

ARCHIE: I'm not sure if she'll come.

DANNY: *She said* she'll come.

ARCHIE: That doesn't mean she'll come.

DANNY: A person says they'll come they'll come.

ARCHIE: Not necessarily.

Pause.

DANNY: Why *shouldn't* she come?

ARCHIE: She might have been being polite.

DANNY: No.

ARCHIE: She might have been too embarrassed to say 'no'.

DANNY: No.

ARCHIE: She might have thought we were lonely.

DANNY: No. (We're *not* lonely.)

ARCHIE: She might have thought we were *desperate*.

Pause.

DANNY: We're not lonely. We live together.

ARCHIE: Well, Danny.

DANNY: What Archie?

ARCHIE: Sometimes I'm lonely.

Pause.

Anyway:/

DANNY: So she says she'll come, she'll come.

ARCHIE: She said she'd phone if she wasn't coming.

DANNY: Oh well then:/ . . .

ARCHIE: Oh well then what?

DANNY: Oh well then *she'll phone if she's not coming.*

ARCHIE: Not necessarily.

DANNY: Yes.

ARCHIE: No.

DANNY: A person says they'll phone to say they're not coming, a person/

ARCHIE: She might have been being polite.

DANNY: She might be too embarrassed to come.

DANNY: No.

ARCHIE: Yes. Too embarrassed to come *at all.*

Pause.

DANNY: Why should she be too embarrassed to come *at all*?

ARCHIE: She might not have fancied *you.*

DANNY: Pardon?

ARCHIE: She might have thought she had to sleep with you.

DANNY: What?

ARCHIE: Even though it was me she fancied. (Obviously.)

DANNY: Eh?

ARCHIE: She might have thought I was procuring her for you.

DANNY: Haw wait a minute.

ARCHIE: Because procurement is probably the only way an ugly charmless bastard like you could get anything.

DANNY: Oh but Archie.

ARCHIE: And she probably worried because she'd be too embarrassed to say no to the procurement after we'd invited her round and given her a cake. (What?)

DANNY: Why does she have to sleep here *at all*?

ARCHIE: Because I want her to sleep here.

DANNY: Why?

ARCHIE: Because I want her to sleep here *with me.*

Pause.

DANNY: That's not fair.

ARCHIE: I want her to sleep here with me because: *sometimes I'm lonely.*

DANNY: Because if she has to sleep here I'd like us all to sleep together.

Pause.
Phone rings.
They don't answer it.

What did you say it meant again if the phone rings?

ARCHIE: It means she's ringing up to say she's not coming.

DANNY picks up the knife to cut the cake.

Don't.

DANNY: Why not?

ARCHIE: Don't!

DANNY: I was going to cut the cake in two.

ARCHIE: Don't.

DANNY: Why not?

ARCHIE: Because I *don't want* any.

Pause.
DANNY puts the knife down.

DANNY: Yes, but what do you mean, you're lonely?

Phone continues to ring as lights fade.

A WHOLLY HEALTHY GLASGOW

A Wholly Healthy Glasgow was first performed at the Royal Exchange Theatre, Manchester on 29 January 1987. It was revived for the Edinburgh Festival 1987 and then played at the Royal Court Theatre, London in 1988. The cast was as follows:

DONALD DICK	Tom Watson
CHARLEY HOOD	Gerard Kelly
MURDO CALDWELL	Paul Higgins

Directed by   Richard Wilson
Designed by   Sue Plummer

Set
The massage chambers of the Spartan Health Club, Glasgow. The stage has three exits.

Note on Layout
The mark / indicates an interruption:

1) when a character breaks his own train of thought:
> CHARLEY: . . . And. You *couldn't* line yourself a line up. Because let's face it about you Donny, you are nothing but a/ lined *your own* line up? Because for *Fuck's* sake . . . etc.

2) when one character is interrupted by another where:
>   a) the character returns to his own train of thought after the other has finished:
>   DONALD: I didn't say it:/
>   CHARLEY: Because you say I've just gone and/
>   DONALD: I didn't say it:/
>   CHARLEY: You say I've just gone and that leaves me . . . etc.

>   b) the character changes his emphasis or train of thought after the other has finished:
>   CHARLEY: I think that's the/
>   DONALD: That has to be the/
>   CHARLEY: Oh mammy, daddy, it can't be the/
>   DONALD ⎱
>   CHARLEY ⎰   It's the new instructor.

ACT ONE

As the lights come up DONALD *comes in from reception. He carries a small closed circuit monitor. He plugs it in and experiments with locations before settling down to watch it from a swivel chair.*

CHARLEY *comes in from reception.*

CHARLEY: So Donny boy, son. See me.

DONALD: Heh Charley: see you.

CHARLEY: Today I am some kind of good guy.

DONALD: Divert the shite elsewhere, uh? I'm/

CHARLEY: Today I/

DONALD: I'm occupied.

> CHARLEY *takes out cigarette unseen by* DONALD.

> So you've been out, you've been in *all bastarding day.*

CHARLEY: A guy's got to *operate.*

DONALD: Shut up

CHARLEY: A guy's to go out, come in the street to operate.

DONALD: Shut the fuck up.

CHARLEY: Because you go out, you come in the street to operate and you are *well away.* (I am not a time waster),

> CHARLEY *lights cigarette, unseen by* DONALD.

> So Donny boy, son.

DONALD: All I'm wanting's/

CHARLEY: So *don't* look at us.

DONALD: All I'm wanting's *decapitation plans for the new boy.*

CHARLEY: So the day's all going *my* way.

DONALD: Plans for/

CHARLEY: All *our* way.

DONALD: Plans for *the new instructor.*

> DONALD *turns sharply to* CHARLEY. CHARLEY *conceals cigarette.*

CHARLEY: So there's time the morrow for the new boy.

DONALD: Aye no there's not.

CHARLEY: And don't hatchet my happiness.

DONALD: Aye but/

CHARLEY: Because *don't remind me* about the new boy.

DONALD: Bobby phoned up!

> CHARLEY *takes a puff.*

CHARLEY: Did that prick and a half Bobby want?

DONALD: So plans the night, right?

CHARLEY: And. I will bend the earholes to your heavy jobbying breath about the new boy, *the morrow.*

DONALD: *The night.*

CHARLEY: Ach aye: the night. (If there's time.)

DONALD: There's *going to be* time. (Four jobbying hours till we shut.)

CHARLEY: *As long* as there's time.

DONALD: There's time *definitely.* (The new boy starts *the morrow.*)

CHARLEY: A guy's to get time to *operate.* (The morrow?)

DONALD: The morrow.

CHARLEY: *Does the new boy fuck* start the morrow. Starts *Tuesday.*

DONALD: Bobby *phoned up!*

> CHARLEY *takes a puff.*

CHARLEY: So fuck's the new boy starting the morrow for?

DONALD: So plans the night.

CHARLEY: The new boys *always* start Tuesday.

DONALD: Because we/

CHARLEY: And. The morrow's Monday.

DONALD: We have got to plan.

CHARLEY: The new boys *always* get their first day *off.*

DONALD: Plan to *get rid* of the new boy.

CHARLEY: They always get *the Monday* off.

DONALD: A bastarding, *interfering* new boy.

CHARLEY: The Monday off after the ten day two weekend initiation training course at Pontefract.

DONALD: So plans the night, right?

CHARLEY: Pontefract jobbying head office.

DONALD: Because no plans to get rid of the new instructor and/ and/ . . . (I'm occupied.)

DONALD *adjusts closed circuit.*

CHARLEY: What's this new boy's name?

DONALD: I don't kow.

CHARLEY: Didn't you ask

DONALD: No.

CHARLEY: Didn't Bobby say?

DONALD: Did he fuck . . . Because I don't care.

CHARLEY: Neither do I. (Fuck.)

Pause.

But you kill me. So ra ha ha. Aye ra ha ha and today's been kind of *ecstatic* this far. (Fact: I say to God: 'Heh go easy with the glee you free-handed basket you,' I says. He says: 'Fuck off pleb. You're *getting* your glee. So lie down be genuinely delirous, OK?') So Donny: you're joining in the joy, boy. And. There's a fly man waiting for me at the bar, the Empire Hotel with a fur coat. (Ta ra).

DONALD: A fur coat's fuck all use *to me.*

CHARLEY: The fur coat's *not for you.*

DONALD: So don't tell us about the bastard.

CHARLEY: It's for Alana.

ALANA (*off, on tannoy*). If Mr McGuigan is in the gym, would he come to reception, please? We have a telephone call for you.

CHARLEY: Aye ra ha ha, Donny. So let me just *listen* to my Alana. *Listen*? Let me just *look* at my Alana.

CHARLEY *goes to closed circuit screen.*

So switch up to reception.

DONALD: Och/

CHARLEY *forcibly adjusts closed circuit.*

ALANA (*off, on tannoy*): If Mr McGuigan is in the gym, would he come to reception, please? We have a telephone call for you.

CHARLEY: So. That's my Alana. And she sits up at reception. Aye, that's my Alana and take over reception from her, uh, Donny?

DONALD: Och I'm all right here.

CHARLEY: Do us a favour, the once.

DONALD: I'm all right *as I am.*

DONALD *adjusts closed circuit.*

CHARLEY: So come on to fuck, Donny. The fly man might take a walk I'm not back to him before six. And. Because: the Alana's to *try the fur coat on* at the bar, the Empire Hotel. I mean: she's a jobbying beauty and she likes to swank in mink. (I don't mind). So she *likes* to try stuff on. (Because she is only a human cunt). And. We go about together trying on *all sorts* of the bastards till I'm fucked and she's happy.

DONALD: So you take her about, she tries stuff on, you pay?

CHARLEY: Oh ho now Donny: the Alana!

DONALD: You big soft cunt you.

CHARLEY: You must be joking and you *definitely* must be joking. She goes about with me, she tries stuff on, *nobody* pays. Because the Alana, me are 'the gruesome bastarding twosome'. (Ta ra).

CHARLEY *takes a puff.*

I mean Donny: I would hardly go about with her if she was a prick. (Consult your nut, uh?). *She*, aye *she* gets to swagger round ten minutes in half a leopard, say 'Piss off shiteface, I'm not buying it' to the flyman, she's happy. See her: she'd give her manicured jobbying toenails to perspire in ermine at the bar, the Empire Hotel. So Donny boy: do the favour, uh? (I'm laughing for you.)

CHARLEY *goes to take a puff.*
DONALD *slowly turns to look at* CHARLEY. CHARLEY *hides his cigarette.* DONALD *turns away again.* CHARLEY *goes to take a puff.*

DONALD: Get that fag out.

CHARLEY *chokes.*

Because what have I told you about smoking in my massage chambers?

CHARLEY *chokes louder.*

I've got my atmosphere to think about.

CHARLEY *chokes louder, loses cigarette.*

And when my good shagpile comes back down here no more cigarette ends are getting stubbed out in it, OK?

CHARLEY *calms down, stubs cigarette out.*

OK?

CHARLEY: What are you looking at?

DONALD: None of your business.

CHARLEY: Because what *are* you looking at?

DONALD: Never you mind.

CHARLEY: Because whatever you're looking at/

CHARLEY *leaps forward and spins* DONALD*'s chair.*

You can't see it now.

DONALD: Bastard you . . . Because this stops . . . this stops . . . and I'll/ I'll/

Chair stops.

I'm occupied.

DONALD *adjusts closed circuit.*

CHARLEY: So Donny: Have I got some beauty of a punter coming in. Coming in any minute. And. This is it. So you hold on to the punter at reception for me ten minutes and I'll line the punter up for you. (Ta ra.)

DONALD: I might not be needing your punter.

CHARLEY: Suspend the wank.

DONALD: I might not be needing your line up.

CHARLEY: You're *wanting* the line up, you're *getting* the line up, you'll be *jobbying grateful* for the line up.

CHARLEY *takes a puff.*

So/

DONALD: I might have my own punter.

CHARLEY: I'm laughing for you. (What?)

DONALD: My own line up.

CHARLEY: And that *will be right.*

DONALD: And this punter I might have is *brilliant looking.*

DONALD *adjusts closed circuit.*

CHARLEY: Well ra ha ha. Aye ra ha ha and don't *come* it. *Have you fuck* lined yourself up a line up. Because that's not the arrangement. And. You *couldn't line yourself up a line up. Because let's face it about you Donny, you are nothing but a/ lined your own* line up? Because for *fucks* sake . . .

CHARLEY *takes a puff.*

And. Now. But. Donny my boy, son. See fucking here. Time to acquaint ourselves the *bastarding business* aspect, eh? So last day the month's the day. And. Club's £100 short the break even. And. Meaning. I'm £100 short my bonus. And. So my bonus is not shiting much. (I can forego that bastard, no bother.) And. But we get by the break even we keep jobbying Bobby quiet. (A fact or a falsehood?) And. Meaning: We catch this certain to renew his membership beauty of a bastarding renewal punter due in any minute. And. Because he's *the only* certain-to-renew-his membership beauty of a bastarding renewal punter's going to barge in with a cheque book all night. And. We get by the break even if it stops Bobby coming from Pontefract. And. Because Bobby coming from Pontefract puts the boot *right up* all that you, me have built up together over the years. (Am I right, am I wrong?) And. So howsabout just holding on to my giant jobby of a certain to renew his membership beauty of a bastarding renewal punter ten minutes at reception for us, uh? Alana, me'll be trying on a couple of patched up badgers. So I'll see she doesn't exceed a swagger round the bar, the Empire Hotel in them. And. So ra ha ha and nip back in here, so I will, pin down the renewal boy and knock the cash up by the break even. (Brilliant arrangement, uh?) And. Who's Bobby think he's kidding? Because I says to Bobby. I says: 'No chance breaking even in August, Bobby. Glasgow's evacuated to the Costa Brava. Glasgow's eyeing up suntanned talent out a hotel balcony telescope at Corfu. Glasgow's chucking up Paella down a Majorcan stank.'

Pause.

And he listen? He fuck. And. So take over reception from my Alana, uh?

DONALD: *How come* you want the Alana *off* the reception?

CHARLEY: The fur coat, *I says.*

DONALD: Fur coat and be fucked. Because *you* can take over the reception, the Alana.

CHARLEY: Aye and *oh* no.

DONALD: The Alana'll be making it to the bar, the Empire Hotel *on her own.*

CHARLEY: Oh no *definitely.*

DONALD: Because Bobby phoned up.

CHARLEY: So?

DONALD: And Bobby's phoning back.

CHARLEY: Oh? . . . And?

DONALD: He's phoning *you* back.

CHARLEY: Me?

DONALD: In *five* minutes.

CHARLEY: What's he phoning me/? (Five?) I says to you: *Always* inform the prick I've *just* gone.

DONALD: I always do say: 'He's *just* gone, Mr Bybugger.' (Normally.)

CHARLEY: So *keep* saying it.

DONALD: Why should I? (Fuck.)

CHARLEY: Why *didn't* you say it?

DONALD: I didn't say it:/

CHARLEY: Because you say I've just gone and/

DONALD: I didn't say it:/

CHARLEY: You say I've just gone and that leaves me thirty minutes from the time he phones up.

DONALD: I didn't say it/ the *deplorable bastarding abuse* I've to take from you. I mean: you've been out, you've been in all fucking day. You've been out, you've been in, instead of standing up the front door grabbing in the punters off the street to *line me up.*

Pause.

CHARLEY: So. You lined *yourself* up a punter? Because *fuck you.* I line you up your punters for the massage. I line you up punters for the après-massage, giving you the wee nod on all them that are 'likely'. And. So the way things are going around here you'll be wanting back your fair share the sales commission money next, by God. Haw. I don't get *far more* than my fair share the sales commission money I walk the streets. You any idea the expense of my life style? (I am a guy gets tanked up on champagne cocktails.)

DONALD: I don't give a fuck the sales commission money. I don't give a fuck *any* money. (Some wee bastards like me are above all that.) For I line myself up a punter the massage converts to the après-massage, what the fuck is it to you? Pricks like you lack dignity. I'm occupied.

CHARLEY: You've never lined yourself up a punter *before.* (Donny.)

DONALD: Because when's the last time *you* lined me up a punter?

CHARLEY: It's August.

DONALD: Ignorant cunt.

CHARLEY: August, *I says.*

DONALD: When's the last time you lined me up a punter's going to lie down, *convert* to the après-massage?

CHARLEY: It's August. (Fuck.) When's the last time a punter walked in here for me to line you up?

Pause. CHARLEY takes out, lights, a cigarette.

So where *is* Bobby?

DONALD: I/

CHARLEY: Pontefract head office, I presume?

DONALD: I don't know.

CHARLEY: You not hear a scabby Yorkshire accent the background?

DONALD: I don't kow, *I says.*

CHARLEY: And you're totally certain the fly bampot's not sitting round the corner the bar, the Empire Hotel?

DONALD: I'm occupied.

Pause.

CHARLEY: So you told Bobby I'd be back in five minutes, uh? So I jump out the door more than five minutes and what happens to me? What happens to *me*? What happens to *us*? Because I am out the door more a regulation thirty minutes and Bobby finds out, Bobby does not put the boot in at me. (I am indispensable big money around here.) *Oh* no. He does not put the boot in at me: he comes from Pontefract.

DONALD: You better hope he *doesn't* come from Pontefract.

CHARLEY: And he comes from Pontefract *you* stand to lose.

DONALD: Because he comes from Pontefract and I get booted, what other soft cunt sent in take my place would let you take *far more* your share the sales prospects?

CHARLEY: Because Bobby will *not* turn the blind eye.

DONALD: Bobby will make fuck all difference to me.

CHARLEY: Bobby will not turn the blind eye to the après-massage. (What?)

DONALD: Fuck all difference. (By the way.) Because I don't get any après-massage. (Do I?)

Pause.

CHARLEY: So you *definitely* told Bobby I'd be back in five minutes?

DONALD: Definitely, Charley. (So I did.)

CHARLEY: Jesus fucking God Donny that's me *stuck here*.

CHARLEY *takes a puff.*

So Donny: *you'll* have to take Alana the bar, the Empire Hotel.

DONALD: Och away chase your jobby round a U-bend, Charley. I'm occupied.

DONALD *adjusts closed circuit.*

And get that cigarette out. (I've got my shagpile to think about.)

CHARLEY *goes to take another puff, but interrupts himself:*

CHARLEY: Your *shagpile*? I wish you'd take your shagpile and – Heh wait a minute. Where *is* your shagpile?

DONALD: Upstairs.

CHARLEY: Because is that you *hiding* your shagpile?

DONALD: It's drying out upstairs, *I said.*

CHARLEY: Your fucking stupid-looking shagpile.

DONALD: That shagpile was given to me by an admirer.

CHARLEY: Oh for fuck's sake: 'an admirer'.

DONALD: An admirer out of my heyday.

CHARLEY *takes a puff.*

And get that cigarette *out*, I says . . . Because you've been out, you've been in all jobbying day. Instead of helping me wash and handpick 48 cigarette ends *out* my shagpile.

DONALD *produces and gives to* CHARLEY *a goldfish bowl crammed with cigarette ends.* CHARLEY *takes a puff and flicks ash into it.*

CHARLEY: Aye ra ha ha, you kill me. And. So what's this: 'I don't get any après-massage.'?

DONALD: I don't!

CHARLEY: How come you're sitting waiting a punter the now then?

DONALD: Aye one wee punter maybe.

CHARLEY: You enterprising geriatric fuck you.

DONALD: One's not enough but. Because I need my nooky. And I need my nooky on a *daily bastarding basis*. I mean: I am not a leper or an ornament on a mantlepiece.

DONALD *adjusts closed circuit.*

CHARLEY: So Donny boy, son: see this punter of yours. What does this punter of yours do for a living?

DONALD: Never you mind.

CHARLEY: What's his *career*?

DONALD: Because I'm not telling *you*.

CHARLEY: Because I have often heard you say the career can add the dash of spice to the après-massage., (Am I right, am I wrong?) . . . So what is your punter's career? Because *my* punter's career is:

professional jobbying footballer. (Ta ra.)

CHARLEY *takes a puff.*

And. So don't batter me with joy, Donny. Because the name of my punter *is*: Craigie Stein. *Oh* aye: Craigie Stein *himself.* Craigie Stein, the big time international footballer. (Ta ra.)

CHARLEY *takes a blatant puff, puts cigarette out into goldfish bowl and puts it down.*

DONALD: Don't kid.

CHARLEY: Aye!

DONALD: Not *the* Craigie Stein.

CHARLEY: Craigie Stein *himself*!

DONALD: Don't come it, uh? Because international footballers don't sign up at back alley health joints.

CHARLEY: I know they don't. Of course they don't. I thought this *myself* until the cunt staggered in here Thursday night *steaming drunk*, aye steaming drunk and a battered in kneecap. And. Because, oh yes: Craigie Stein's the mental bampot had his kneecap well jobbied a year ago. And. His kneecap has not recuperated. And. So his club has given the boy the boot. And. Therefore I stepped right up to Craigie Stein sold him the buy-now-cheap-rate-new-enrolment special at £200 for the year. Oh aye: I sold the poor certain-to-go-bankrupt bastard *his hope.* And. He'll be in again any minute I'm hitting him a buy-now-cheap-rate-early-*renewal* special at £150 for the *second* year. (Taking me *right by* the break even.) . . . So you *taking* the Alana the bar, the Empire Hotel for us? . . . (I'll *definitely* line you up the Craigie Stein.) . . . Because engage the doll with alcohol a half an hour, uh? Tell her I'll pick her up later. And. So that an agreement?

CHARLEY *takes out cigarette packet. Discovers it is empty. Throws it away.*

DONALD: How come you want the Alana off reception?

CHARLEY: The fur coat, *I says.*

DONALD: So I take her the bar, the Empire Hotel and she tries on the fur coats?

CHARLEY: No.

DONALD: No?

CHARLEY: I mean: *no*! Because the fur coats are not important. I mean: I'll see to the fur coats later, OK?

Pause.

DONALD: So why *do* you want the Alana off reception?

CHARLEY: Why/? What is this? The fur/ Can we talk about this later? . . . Because come on to fuck the Craigie'll *be* here.

DONALD: *Why*?

CHARLEY: Because the Craigie's *due.*

DONALD:*Why*?

CHARLEY: Because . . . Because I hope this is the last tanking my wee pride has to take. *Oh* aye . . . Because the fur-coat story was a pack of brilliant lies, I thought up. (Ta ra.) . . . But it fooled you, uh?

DONALD: Did it fuck.

CHARLEY: It fooled you however?

DONALD: I knew it was jobby from the kick off.

CHARLEY: Is that right? So ra ha ha. Aye ra ha ha, Donny. So the Alana sees the footballer she turns the head. She turns the head and Charley suffers. So Charley makes sure with assistance off his bestmates Alana *doesn't* turn the head. Because see the Alana, right? Alana goes for any guy gets his name the paper going. So say the Alana's sitting my taxi one night. I'm paying for it, back to *my* place. We're well bevvied up, I paid for it, not that I mind. I stop the taxi at one point, I pick up a paper. She reads it, I paid for it, not that I mind *definitely*. So the Alana sees a guy out the street. A guy out the street she says got his name the paper: the paper *she's reading.* So the Alana stops the taxi, gets out, *picks the other guy up.* (Some bird her, uh?) Meanwhile I'm left sitting our taxi, paying our taxi, paying *her share* our taxi, not that I mind. And. So I look the paper, I see this other guy, the guy the street, the guy got his name the paper, got his name the paper for flashing his dick. See what I mean about Alana? (Fuck.)

Pause.

DONALD: Why can't you get casual about tit?

Pause.

CHARLEY: Because why can't you get casual about cock? (Is why.)

Pause.

DONALD: So this Craigie Stein's on for me?

CHARLEY: Oh he's *on* for you.

DONALD: You really think so, Charley?

CHARLEY: On for you, no bother, Donny. Because I'll say to him: 'See that wee massage therapist shite, Donald Dick, right? See him: he's an answer to a fucked-up international footballer's prayer' . . . So you're *wanting* me to line you him up?

DONALD: Aye. Oh *aye* . . . Because the gorgeous bastard's got shoulders wide as a corporation bus.

Pause.

CHARLEY: Aye ra ha, you kill me. And. What about your own punter?

DONALD: Oh my own punter isn't definite. But I'll manage both of them. If necessary.

Pause.

CHARLEY: So go take the Alana out, uh.

Pause.

DONALD: And plans get to get rid the new boy the night, Charley?

CHARLEY: Plans the night?

DONALD: *The night.*

CHARLEY: Because come on to/ Oh aye. The night. (Fuck.) The night, *definitely.*

DONALD *turns back to closed circuit.*

DONALD: Because the new boy's supposed to be a keen wee cunt.

CHARLEY: So you take the Alana out the road and I definitely hold the Craigie for you. (Keen?)

DONALD: Keen, so Bobby says.

CHARLEY: Keen *will* be right. Aye, keen to cream off my best sales, my best *renewal* prospects maybe.

DONALD: Bobby says the new *volunteered* to start a day early.

CHARLEY: The bright wee shite's not screwing me.

DONALD: (The morrow). Haw heh: who's the dick down the gym?

CHARLEY: So *take* the Alana, uh? (What?)

CHARLEY *looks at the screen.*

No cunt I know.

DONALD: And the body of a stallion too.

CHARLEY: So *go!*

DONALD: He's limped off the screen.

CHARLEY: Go! (Limped?) Take a/

DONALD: It's the international footballer.

CHARLEY: Take a jobby. The international footballer's not due *yet.* (Not *just* yet.) I mean: switch over/ (You'd not time to see.) Switch over the changing rooms.

DONALD *adjusts closed circuit.*

No. Switch to up reception.

DONALD *adjusts closed circuit.*

No. Switch back down the guym.

DONALD *adjusts closed circuit.*

DONALD: Maybe the footballer came early.

CHARLEY: He wouldn't come early.

DONALD: He was drunk but.

CHARLEY: I *don't let* my punters come early.

DONALD: He was *drunk* Thursday, you talked to him. He was drunk, so he fails to understand: 'Don't for *fuck's* sake, come early.'

CHARLEY: So Donny:/

DONALD: What, Charley?

CHARLEY: The tool came early.

Pause.

DONALD: So who's the object with him?

CHARLEY: Heh: who's that measuring the leg?

DONALD: The *inside* leg.

CHARLEY: I think that's the/

DONALD: That has to be the/

CHARLEY: Oh mammy, daddy, it can't be the/

DONALD } It's the new instructor.
CHARLEY }

Pause.

CHARLEY: And. Tuesday he/

DONALD: Monday.

CHARLEY: Tuesday *he* starts. (What?)

DONALD: *Bobby said* Monday.

CHARLEY: But this *isn't* Monday.

DONALD: It's Sunday night, my fuck. And Bobby *said* this new boy is *keen.*

CHARLEY: This isn't Monday/ (Keen? Aye: keen with my punter.)

DONALD: *My* line up.

CHARLEY: *Your* line up . . . so I'm *separating* the cunts.

CHARLEY *goes to go.*

DONALD: You're *not* separating them.

CHARLEY: Get to fuck. *Of course* I'm separating them.

DONALD: You separate them, the new boy gets ugly.

CHARLEY: Eh?

DONALD: Ugly in front of our punter.

CHARLEY: Oh aye. (Fuck.) The using bastard.

Pause.

DONALD: Go reception, Charley, get the new boy up *the tannoy.* Bobby always gets the new boys to follow the tannoy.

CHARLEY: OK. (Fuck.)

Pause.

DONALD: And look at *the way* the new boy's measuring him up.

CHARLEY: And I've *already* measured him up.

DONALD: To re-measure a punter has got to be despicable . . . So did you mark his measurements on his card, for all to see?

CHARLEY: Thursday night. The night he joined. Chest and waist.

DONALD: So how come the new boy's measuring him up *again*?

CHARLEY: And. If I see an early-cheap-rate-renewal contract coming out down there I'm/

DONALD: So go, Charley.

CHARLEY *is about to go. Telephone rings.* DONALD *picks it up, listens in and quickly passes it to* CHARLEY.

I'll go reception.

CHARLEY (*to phone*): Spartan Health. May we help you?

DONALD *goes to go.*

Well hello, Mr Bybugger.

DONALD *goes out to reception.*

Yes, Mr Bybugger.

Pause.

No, Mr Bybugger.

DONALD (*off, on tannoy*): Instructor to the massage chambers. Instructor to the massage chambers. Thanking you.

CHARLEY: Yes, Mr Bybugger . . . grand, fine.

DONALD: Would the instructor in the gym proceed to the massage chambers?

CHARLEY: Oh yes, grand, fine.

Pause.

And what's the new instructor's name by the way, Mr Bybugger?

DONALD: The *new* instructor to the massage chambers, please. *Now*, please. Thanking you.

CHARLEY: Murdo . . . Murdo Caldwell, Mr Bybugger? . . . Fine, grand, Mr Bybugger.

DONALD: Would the new instructor *kindly* leave what he is doing and go to the massage chambers?

CHARLEY: No, no. The early arrival of a new instructor *suits us fine*, Mr Bybugger.

DONALD: Instructor to the massage chambers. Immediately. Thanking you.

CHARLEY: Oh grand, fine. No. No problem, Mr Bybugger. Yes, Mr Bybugger, certainly. Thanking you.

CHARLEY *puts phone down. He looks at closed circuit.*

Unbelievable ignorant cunt.

DONALD *comes in from reception, in haste.*

DONALD: Unbelievable bent basket.

CHARLEY: And./

DONALD: Heh:/

CHARLEY: So he *ignores* the calls.

DONALD: Heh Charley:/

CHARLEY: While he gives the bampot in the gym the measuring tape treatment.

DONALD: She's not there, Charley.

CHARLEY: Imagine ignoring the calls. (What?) Cunts like that have *definitely* lost the place. Because/ (What?)

DONALD: The Alana's went.

CHARLEY: Lost the bastarding place. She's not *went* (fuck), she's/

DONALD: She's went.

CHARLEY: She's went? Haw heh: 'went' went home or 'went' went to the lavvy?

DONALD: She's *went*!

Pause. CHARLEY goes to closed circuit and checks.

CHARLEY: So. Going straight down the gym, uh? And. Ignoring the tannoy announcements! Because *oh* no. This cannot be overlooked in a miniature vomit like the new boy, like 'Murdo Caldwell'. Because oh *yes*: if the Alana has went and viewed that stud with a limp *before* she went, she'd've *definitely* turned the head. And Donny: the new instructor's getting booted *the night*.

DONALD: Plans the night, booted the morrow.

CHARLEY: Booted the night now, it'll have to be. Because Bobby phoned up. And. He's coming the morrow. And. We are not being seen slicing a hammer through the new boy's nut in front of Bobby. (Fuck.) So we boot the bampot the night and you happy, Donny? You happy?

Pause. DONALD turns to CHARLEY.

DONALD: I'm happy.

CHARLEY *goes to go.*

But separate them gently down there, OK?

CHARLEY: OK. (Because Gentle is my middle bastarding name.)

CHARLEY *goes to go and thinks better of it.*

So Donny: I send Murdo up here, keep him quiet ten minutes, I'll get back up boot the cunt. *Meanwhile* I renew the punter, line him up for you. OK?

DONALD: OK.

CHARLEY: So put it there, uh?

DONALD: No.

CHARLEY: Eh? How come?

DONALD: Because I'm not putting it nowhere . . . If anyone's putting it anywhere you're putting it here.

Pause. CHARLEY goes to DONALD and shakes his hand.

DONALD: Thanks.

CHARLEY: That's OK.

DONALD: And thanks for putting out your bastarding disgusting cigarette.

CHARLEY: That's OK, too.

DONALD: Big of you . . . oh and heh Charley.

CHARLEY: What's that, Donny?

DONALD: The Alana left a note.

Pause.

(So she did.)

Pause.

She'll phone you later.

Pause. CHARLEY goes to go and thinks better of it.

CHARLEY: So the Alana phones in and I am with the renewal punter, enquire as to the bastarding location, the bastarding Alana, uh? (Fuck.) And. Don't think I stopped smoking for you. (I stop smoking for *nobody*. People *start* smoking for *me*.) I ran out of bastarding *cigarettes*.

DONALD turns away.
CHARLEY goes out to gym.
Telephone. DONALD picks it up.

DONALD: Spartan Health. May we help you?

Pause.

He's just walked out Alana.

Pause.

With a client, Alana.

Pause.

Not get him for you, no?

MURDO *comes in from the gym.*
MURDO *sees* DONALD, *he gestures apology and he goes to go.*

DONALD (*to* MURDO): Stay.
(*To phone*:) Someone here Alana, OK?
(*To* MURDO:) OK?
(*To phone*:) Aye. A nice night to you.

DONALD *replaces the phone.*

MURDO: Do you work here?

DONALD: I do.

Pause.

Heh:/

MURDO: Well I don't think he was right.
(Sorry).

DONALD: Hey you:/ (What?)

MURDO: An instructor came right up and
interrupted me.

DONALD: Well for a/

MURDO: When I was *half way through* a
company procedure.

DONALD: For a start you're/

MURDO: Then he sent me up here.

DONALD: You're/

MURDO: Could I have done something
wrong?

DONALD: You're/

MURDO: But I was half way through the
company procedure for *newly-enrolled
members.*

DONALD: You're not supposed to be here
yet.

Pause.

MURDO: Oh ah Mr Bybugger *said* I could
come early. (Sorry.)

DONALD: *This* early?

MURDO: He didn't say *how* early.

DONALD: He told *us* early meant
tomorrow.

MURDO: Oh ah should I go home?

DONALD: And. (What?) No!

MURDO: I *could* go home, if I *had* to. And
come back tomorrow.

DONALD: You're going nowhere.

MURDO: I *wouldn't mind* if it's *wrong* of
me to be here. (What, sorry?)

DONALD: You *don't* leave a place, you've
just arrived . . . Do you?

MURDO: Oh ah no. (Sorry.) I mean;
thanks. Because I *don't want* to go home.
(So when I arrived from Pontefract I
came straight here.)

Pause.

DONALD: How come you didn't knock my
door?

MURDO: Pardon, sorry?

DONALD: Because the front of that door
says 'private'.

MURDO: Oh, ah the other instructor told
me to come in and wait.

DONALD: We knock doors here.

MURDO: Should I have knocked anyway?
(Sorry.)

DONALD: Plus/

MURDO: Because Mr Bybugger didn't
mention knocking doors.

DONALD: How come you didn't answer
the tannoy calls?

MURDO: Oh ah I couldn't. I/ Because Mr
Bybugger says a new member's first visit
takes priority over a tannoy call.

Pause.

I can smell cigarette smoke.

DONALD: I doubt it.

MURDO: I'm sure I can smell cigarette
smoke.

DONALD: Because no one smokes in here.

Pause.

How come you didn't want to go home?

MURDO: Oh, ah I can't/ I mean I prefer
not to discuss it if that's all right. (Sorry).

DONALD: Please yourself.

MURDO: But it was also my enthusiasm
which made me come early. (I have been
told I've got a *lot* of enthusiasm.) . . .

Where would the other instructor have gone to with the new member?

DONALD: The fuck should I know.

MURDO: Because the instructor escorted the member *right out of the gym.*

DONALD: Renewing the cunt's membershp?

MURDO: Even though he was only *half-way through* his first visit. (Pardon?)

DONALD: He'll be flogging the bastard an early-cheap-rate renewal.

MURDO: Oh, ah but doesn't he know that Mr Bybugger says you can't offer an early-cheap-rate renewal until the *sixth* visit?

DONALD: I know fuck all about it.

MURDO: By which time the member has had results and is able *to see* the advantages of the early-cheap-rate renewal. (What?)

DONALD: I says: fuck all do I know about it.

MURDO: Oh ah *why?*

DONALD: Because I *don't do* any renewals.

Pause.

MURDO: I'm sure I can smell cigarette smoke.

DONALD: No.

MURDO: It smells *very like* cigarette smoke.

DONALD: Because I don't permit smoking in here.

Pause.

MURDO: Why don't you do any renewals?

DONALD: Because I am not a greedy, money-grabbing bastard . . . You were *thorough* the way you measured up that member.

MURDO: Oh ah. How did you see me? (Sorry) I mean: can I ask?

DONALD *points to closed circuit.*

DONALD: *Too* thorough.

MURDO: Oh ah Mr Bybugger says you're not supposed to look at the closed circuit.

DONALD: (Not him again.)

MURDO: Because the closed circuit monitor is to be kept at reception and used for security checks only. I mean: I did ask Mr Bybugger a question on security checks during the ten-day initiation training-course at Pontefract.

DONALD: OK. So Charley Hood, we are doing a routine security check. So we saw you on the screen. We didn't know *who the hell you were.* We took one look at you and we knew we didn't know you.

MURDO: If you didn't know it was me why did you say 'New instructor to reception' on the tannoy? (Sorry.)

DONALD: We're brilliant guessers.

Pause.

MURDO: Well I didn't know you didn't know/ I'm not blaming *you.* You obviously *didn't know* I got *permission* to go to the gym.

DONALD: *Permission?* Permission who from?

MURDO: The receptionist.

DONALD: The receptionist?

MURDO: The girl.

DONALD: Alana? Because 'the receptionist' and fuck off. You see the man in charge, you see *Charley Hood* before you act.

MURDO: I got permission.

DONALD: Bobby would not like to know he has employed a total tit. (Permission from the receptionist!)

Pause.

MURDO: Well are you completely sure no one has been smoking here?

DONALD: I'm sure as fuck.

MURDO: Oh well oh sorry.

DONALD: Pardon?

MURDO: I mean: sorry if I offended you.

DONALD: What?

MURDO: Sorry if I offended you by not knocking your door.

DONALD: Offended me?

MURDO: Or if I offended you by choosing not to discuss my family background.

DONALD: Offended *me?*

MURDO: Or if I offended you by asking if you worked here.

DONALD: I don't take offence.

MURDO: When I first arrived here/ Pardon?

DONALD: The life I've had. It's made a brass-necked basket out of me. *I've* had *six* ambulances in *one week*, in my time. (Offended?)

MURDO: Well when I first arrived I did ask you if you worked here.

DONALD: Aye, the fuck you do that for?

MURDO: You haven't got the Spartan Health company track suit on. (Sorry.)

Pause.

DONALD: I'm a masseur, *I says.*

MURDO: Oh ah/

DONALD: So I don't need a Spartan Health track suit.

MURDO: What does massage do? (Exactly, sorry.) I mean: are you *allowed* to not wear a track suit?

Pause.

DONALD: So why *did you* measure that client so thoroughly?

MURDO: Oh ah/

DONALD: Why did you measure that client's *inside leg*?

MURDO: He's a new member.

DONALD: He'd *already been* measured. Measured the day he joined. Charley measured him and marked it on his card.

MURDO: Only the chest and waist had been measured.

DONALD: The chest and waist is all that we measure.

MURDO: Mr Bybugger said everyone had to be fully measured.

DONALD: This is a busy club.

MURDO: To create uniformity.

DONALD: At a busy club we measure the chest, the waist only, OK?

MURDO: But the gym was empty. (Sorry.)

DONALD: But from tomorrow:/

MURDO: I had *plenty of time* to measure him fully.

DONALD: Tomorrow Glasgow gets back from Tenerife.

MURDO: But the gym *wasn't* busy.

DONALD: The gym *gets* busy. September starts tomorrow.

Pause.

MURDO: That's great, isn't it, Mr Dick? I mean: *how* busy does it get?

DONALD: *Too busy.*

MURDO: Yes, Mr Bybugger warned me. He said: 'Our Glasgow branch is hard work. But you *can* achieve.'

Pause.

And would you *recommend* massage, Mr Dick?

DONALD: Eh? (Oh *no*. Would I fuck.)

MURDO: What, for instance, would be the role of massage in the health of the body?

DONALD: (Because fuck off.)

MURDO: Because the ten-day initiation training-course at Pontefract didn't include massage.

I'm sure I can smell/ How would I go about *contacting* Mr Bybugger? I mean if I wanted to. (Pardon, sorry.)

DONALD *gestures to telephone.*

He said if I ever wanted to talk over a problem. (*Where*, sorry?)

DONALD (*gesturing to telephone*): Here, reception, *where* you want. (Fuck.)

MURDO: And I do *have* a problem.

DONALD: Do you *want to* phone Bobby?

MURDO: It's to find out *exactly when* I may renew a member. (For instance.)

DONALD: Because sometimes these nice bosses give it a nice touch: They go: 'Phone me with your problems.'

MURDO: But Mr Bybugger *did tell me* exactly when to renew a member.

DONALD: Mr Bybugger is one busy boy.

MURDO: And I might have forgotten. I mean: I *only think* he said six visits.

DONALD: A busy boy does not like to get interrupted.

MURDO: What would Mr Bybugger *do* if he *found out* I'd forgotten what he said, or *even* that I'd *got it wrong?*

Pause.

DONALD: So what is it with you? You some kind of boss's man.? You shouldn't be a boss's man at your age, for fuck's sake. You're only a young wank. I mean I was your age I used to poke a boss's eye out with a bowling pin as soon as look at him. I used to take two-hour tea-breaks, come back tell the cunt I'd have my nooky with a poodle in a cupboard. I mean: fuck me: how come you can't wrap Bobby in kitchen foil, pop him the oven an afternoon? Because see this Bobby, right This Bobby Bybugger thinks he's a perfect specimen? Works out, jogs, eats an immaculate diet? This/ Is all that a fact?

MURDO: Oh ah/

DONALD: Aye well it's *not* a fact. When Bobby is away from home, away from Pontefract he'll eat any old garbage comes his way.

MURDO: Well I watched him in Pontefract. He never left his diet and exercise programme for a second.

DONALD: That's Pontefract. Bobby is away from Pontefract a good half the year his programme gets well fucked. Hamburgers, the lot.

MURDO: In Pontefract/

MURDO *discovers empty cigarette packet.*

DONALD: So my advice to you is get to hell out of it.

MURDO: Oh ah/

Picks up cigarette packet and gives it to DONALD

DONALD: Because you're a really nice guy. (Are you fuck.) Because see these. These belong to Charley Hood. The cunt. Aye. That's the sorry state this place has got *me* into. I was up for the priesthood before I took this job. I wouldn't have dreamed of covering up for a dirty lung-infested bastard like Charley Hood. Oh no.

MURDO: *Where* may I phone Mr Bybugger from?

DONALD: Because, basically, I don't give a fuck. (Phone him where you want.) And if you want to stop *yourself* not giving a fuck get to bastarding hell out of it, before it's too late. At one point I had a twenty-eight inch waist. I've been devastated by Spartan Health and Bobby Bybugger. I mean: I was in London before I came here. Ten scintillating years. Ample nooky, the lot. (Phone him where you want, *I says.*) And see my London pad? It was bastarding *fabulous.* I had chandelier in my kitchenette. Now look at me.

MURDO: I'm phoning Mr Bybugger

DONALD: Don't blame me and he shouts at you.

MURDO: I'm going to clear this up.

DONALD: Don't forget you're *not supposed to be here yet.*

MURDO: Something's *got to be* cleared up. If Mr Bybugger/ I'll *admit* I'm here. If Mr Bybugger/ If I'm *not supposed* to be here Mr Bybugger has a right to shout at me. I *deserve* to be shouted at. But if Mr Bybugger doesn't abide by his diet and exercise programme *I don't want to be here.*

MURDO *goes to phone and thinks better of it.*

I'm phoning Mr Bybugger, *in private.*

MURDO *goes out to reception.*

Pause.

CHARLEY (*off*): Where's that bastard?

CHARLEY *comes on from reception.*

CHARLEY: Bastard.

DONALD *picks up phone.*

Where's that bastard?

DONALD (*to* CHARLEY): Alana phoned up.

CHARLEY: Because I get hold of Murdo and boiling his head will be too good for/ (Alana?)

DONALD: Alana.

Pause.

CHARLEY: Her mother's in a coma?

DONALD *shakes his head and gestures for silence.*

She's at her big Aunty Ruby's? (Oh *no*, man.)

DONALD *shakes his head.*

She's over wee Gina's for a wash and a shave and a character-assassination session?

DONALD *gestures for silence, firmly.*

DONALD (*to phone*); So Murdo. Get off the line, uh? I've got a very urgent business call to make for Mr Bybugger. Buzz up to you, so I will, the line's free, OK?

DONALD *gestures for continued silence, he listens carefully and puts phone down.* DONALD *gives cigarette packet to* CHARLEY *who, not knowing what to do with it, puts it in his pocket.*

CHARLEY: So where is Murdo?

DONALD: Alana's phoning you back later.

CHARLEY: What's he at reception for? (Alana? Phoning *me* back? Fuck's Alana phoning *me* back for?)

DONALD: I don't know.

CHARLEY: You should've got the number. I'd've phoned *her* back. Because *me* phoning *her* back's more my bastarding style.

Pause.

So where did you say she was?

DONALD: I didn't.

CHARLEY: Because where *the fuck* did you say she was? (What?)

DONALD: She didn't forthcome on that.

CHARLEY: So to bastarding fuck you jobbying shite why didn't you *make her* forthcome on that?

Pause.

So what's Murdo at reception for?

DONALD: I got him out the road for you to send me in the footballer. Haw heh wait a minute: *where is* the footballer?

Pause.

CHARLEY: So the Murdo has fucked us up.

DONALD: Where's my line up *I says*?

CHARLEY: So that's/

DONALD: Have you lost me my line up?

CHARLEY: That's Murdo booted the night *definitely.*

DONALD: Because you've lost me my line up you lousy toss off ballhead you. What are you?

Pause.

CHARLEY: *I* didn't lose you the footballer.

DONALD: Oh? So who did?

CHARLEY: Murdo.

DONALD: Murdo?

CHARLEY: Murdo! So you want to see the special-attention treatment Murdo dishes out to the footballer. Because the measurement in detail was *not* the end of it. Oh no. Also *the weight.* Also *the height.* Also the *dietary advice.* Also: the *personalised exercise programme.* I mean: is he under the presumption we are here to *serve the public?* . . .

So the footballer, he goes to himself: how come I didn't get the special-attention treatment the first time I came in, the time I came to enrol, the time Charley Hood took £200 off me measured my chest, my waist in two seconds flat? Because Donny: a place is *inconsistent* to a punter and a punter gets *alert.* And an alert bastarding punter has got an unfair advantage over us. Because an alert bastarding punter is going to *want time* to think the early renewal *over.* (Fuck.)

Pause.

So where is Murdo?

DONALD: Eh? Oh see this Murdo:/

CHARLEY: Because did I hear you say Murdo's phoning Bobby?

DONALD: This Murdo wants to tell Bobby the way things are around here.

CHARLEY: What've you said to Murdo?

DONALD: Because Murdo is a wee boss's man that I have *almost totally* booted for us.

CHARLEY: Because phone calls to Bobby would't've arisen you had kept your gob shut, as I requested. (Fuck.) Because phone calls to Bobby and Bobby *comes from Pontefract.*

DONALD: I *know* he comes from Pontefract. So I *blocked* the phone call to Bobby to give you time to finish Murdo off.

CHARLEY: Phone calls to Bobby shouldn't've arisen. I mean: you get the trust *first*. So you give the new boy a present, you give him a *promise*. Because you give a promise and you create *a feeling of obligation* in the new boy. You create a feeling of obligation and you have thereafter *got his trust*. Because let's face it Donny: you have to get the trust before you can persuade the new boy he's better off fucking off.

Pause.

DONALD: You've lost me my footballer.

CHARLEY: So Donny: did I say we'd *lost* the footballer? Because lost temporarily. Tem-po-ra-ri-ly. So fuck me: this Craigie Stein, right? We're sitting the sales-office he goes: 'I've got a date with a bird.' I went: 'You've got a *bigger* date with yourself, Jim.' He went: 'Oh but I'm not sure.' *This* from a guy with a fucked career, Donny. This from a guy needs his hope. This from a guy with *big* motivation. So I went to him: 'Sign there.' He goes: 'I've got a *date!*' I went: 'A signature costs a second.' He went: 'I want to think about it.' Think about it? So the Murdo *must've* got him alert. Because a mental case with big motivation doesn't *think* about it. A mental case with big motivation *begs* for it.

Pause.

DONALD: Punters walk out *don't* come back.

CHARLEY: This is the exception, Donny.

DONALD: Many's the time you've went to me: 'A punter wants it, a punter buys it *now.*'

CHARLEY: The Craigie does want it but.

DONALD: You've lost me my footballer.

CHARLEY: No Donny. Because I went to him: 'Tonight's *the last* of the early-cheap-rate renewals.' So. He meets the bird, Donny. He meets the bird, she gives him the anti-climax, he'll be back. I mean: the times I've been going out a bird I've went right off she's opened her gob and spoke. Opened her gob and spoke a lot of wank.

So. He meets the bird, she gives him the anti-climax he'll be back. Back deflated and dying to buy. (Ta ra.)

Pause.

DONALD: Well the night, I hope.

CHARLEY: The night.

DONALD: The night, he'll be back.

CHARLEY: The night *I says, definitely.* Because I'm going the bar, the Empire Hotel to *get him.* (*Oh* aye.) So I'll wait his wee bird gives him the anti-climax before I escort him back here his early-cheap-rate renewal. Then it's *over to you,* Donny boy son.

DONALD: Well I hope you find him the night. These empty summer nights in Glasgow are pissing me off. And I've still got my connections in London. I could get my nooky on a regular bastarding basis there.

CHARLEY: Aye ra ha ha cut the London garbage.

DONALD: In fact: you get your nooky every fifteen seconds, the Earl's Court Road.

CHARLEY: I've heard the London garbage before. I've/ Nooky every fifteen seconds, all the same So give me an honorary benthood, for fuck's sake, I'll go to London, too. Because you are one hell of a guy, Donny, the queen should get to meet you. And. I love you *so* much, I wasn't so totally *not* a bent basket I'd get up your couch myself for you.

Pause.

DONALD: So I hope you do find Craigie Stein.

CHARLEY: So do I.

DONALD: I hope you find him, the bar, the Empire Hotel.

CHARLEY: *So do I.*

DONALD: I hope you find him the Alana parked his *smashed-up bastarding kneecap.*

CHARLEY: So do/ heh *wait* a/

DONALD: Because the Alana, the Craigie *could well* have met up reception. (Don't forget.)

CHARLEY: Aye could they? I mean: *could* they? (Fuck.)

CHARLEY *takes out cigarettes. Goes to open them. Remembers.*

I mean: fuck!

DONALD: And you're *not* going the bar, the Empire Hotel, by the way.

CHARLEY: What is this?

DONALD: Because what if Bobby phones back?

CHARLEY: Bobby's *phoned* back.

DONALD: What if Bobby phoned back again?

CHARLEY: Oh fuck aye. Back again. From Pontefract.

DONALD: And if he's *not* phoning you up from Pontefract:/ Because if he's not phoning you up from Pontefract you might just walk into the erratic cunt's face the bar, the Empire Hotel.

Pause.

I could go.

CHARLEY: Pardon?

DONALD: *I* could go look over the bar, the Empire Hotel.

CHARLEY: You could? . . . You could! You go you see Craigie the bar, the Empire Hotel. (And oh God: The Alana. The Alana, the *Craigie*. Oh God.,)

DONALD: So while I'm the bar, the Empire Hotel you'll boot Murdo?

CHARLEY: Murdo?

DONALD: Murdo! You'll boot him so the ugly bastard's *well gone* I get back?

CHARLEY: I'll boot him for you Donny. Put it there.

They shake hands.

DONALD: Because I don't like Murdo.

Pause.

One thing, however: I won't be the bar, the Empire Hotel long, OK?

CHARLEY: OK.

DONALD: The bar, the Empire Hotel is a shitehole.

CHARLEY: *I know* it's a shitehole.

DONALD: It's full of weirdos,/

CHARLEY: So don't be long.

DONALD: Who give me the vomit. So I won't be long, *definitely*.

DONALD *picks up phone.*

DONALD (*to phone*): Murdo? . . . Mr Hood wants a word with you. (*To* CHARLEY): You ready to talk to Murdo, Mr Hood?

CHARLEY: I'm ready, Mr Dick.

DONALD (*to phone*): What? Oh sorry, Murdo son. (*Loud to* CHARLEY): because imagine that, Mr Hood. I went *forgot* to buzz through to Murdo the line to Bobby was free. (*To* MURDO): I'm not sure what he wants to talk about, Murdo. So shoot down here now, OK? . . . Let you try phoning Bobby later.

DONALD *puts phone down.*

So Murdo's *right into* Bobby.

CHARLEY: Nobody's into Bobby. That cunt's too masculine. And, I hope you kept your hands off Murdo's body, by the way.

DONALD: *Murdo's body*?

CHARLEY: Because that's not what sent him upstairs, up phoning Bobby is it?

DONALD: I never considered his body.

CHARLEY: Well get a grip:/

DONALD: Because his *personality* is garbage.

CHARLEY: Because if you *don't* fancy his body you benders are getting far too bastarding fussy.

Knocking.

DONALD: Heh Charley:/

CHARLEY (*shouts*): Hold on.

DONALD: Murdo says he *wasn't* renewing Craigie.

CHARLEY: Fuck *that*.

DONALD: Bobby told him you don't renew until the sixth visit.

CHARLEY: He measured Craigie up it wasn't needed.

DONALD: He measured him because he wasn't happy the way *you* measured him.

Knocking.

CHARLEY: You believe that? Because Murdo might not be able to sell a renewal.

But why jobby about with unreal concepts such as: 'I'm not in it for the money. I'm not in for the nooky. I'm in it for the job satisfaction.'

DONALD: I'm saying what he said.

DONALD *goes out through corridor.*

CHARLEY: Gobble a shite. The purest vomit.

Knocking. CHARLEY *takes out cigarette packet. Goes to open it. Remembers.*

Fuck. (*Shouts, out to* DONALD:) Heh Donny. Buy us a packet of cigarettes, uh?

DONALD (*off*): And you have got to be joking.

Knocking.

CHARLEY (*loud*): Come in. (*Quiet:*) For fuck's sake, *come in.*

MURDO *comes in from reception.*

CHARLEY: Aye Murdo Caldwell? Charley Hood. Couldn't be more pleased to meet you. Couldn't be more pleased your nice early kick-off. How's it going?

MURDO: Oh ah/

CHARLEY: So I couldn't stop introduce myself down the gym there. The matter with the Stein punter was ugent. You saw that, you handled it *dead* professional, *dead* promising.

MURDO: Oh, ah and could I ask a question?

CHARLEY: Ask away. I love a stimulating question. What the fuck is it?

MURDO: Oh and have you time? *You* want to talk to *me.* I mean, *do* you?

CHARLEY: Any amount of time, can I make available, for boys the calibre of you and me. (I like it.) There's calibre in you and me companies the like of Spartan Health are bawling out for. Oh aye man, I watched you from the gym door a couple of wee minutes all impressed, hell of a impressed the gorgeous attention you gave the Stein punter . . .

MURDO: Oh, ah now, what was I/

CHARLEY: He had gratitude on him a mile long. Eh?

MURDO: Oh, ah and what did I say that was so good? (If I can know, I can keep it up.)

CHARLEY: He almost extended his membership. Thanks to you.

MURDO: Oh? *Oh?*

CHARLEY: So I watched you a couple of minutes, all fascinated to fuck.

MURDO: You say what *you* want *first.* (If you want.)

CHARLEY: Aye, well/

MURDO: Ah, oh I mean if you want to ask me mine first, I don't mind.

CHARLEY: OK. So ra ha ha. Aye ra ha ha I'm showing you one of my specials. (They're brilliant.) Because a boy with talent like you:/

MURDO: Oh, ah my *talent?* What's my talent like? (Sorry.) I mean: What's your special for? Oh ah. Is it a 'Spartan Health' special?

CHARLEY: It's better than *that.* (Fuck.)

MURDO: Does Mr Bybugger *not know* about it?

CHARLEY: What am I saying? It's not so much better as *equally* fascinating.

MURDO: Oh ah/

CHARLEY: But if you *don't want* to try my special: I won't be insulted.

Pause.

MURDO: I could try it out, I suppose. I mean: couldn't I? (Sorry.)

CHARLEY: So do you *want* to?

MURDO: Oh, ah OK.

Brilliant. And. Put it there.

They shake hands.

It's a pity, all the same.

MURDO: A pity?

CHARLEY: A pity about your talent.

Pause.

MURDO: Why is it a pity? I mean: what do you mean? (Sorry.)

CHARLEY: I mean, son . . . the total absence of job prospects around here.

MURDO: Pardon?

CHARLEY: Commensurate with your talent.

MURDO: Because the prospects are excellent. (Sorry.)

CHARLEY: And. You'll never be more than a junior gym instructor while I'm the senior gym instructor.

MURDO: I mean: *are* the prospects excellent?

Pause.

I'd like to call Mr Bybugger now.

CHARLEY: Oh, certainly.

MURDO: Did Mr Dick *tell* you about my call to Mr Bybugger?

CHARLEY: Because phone away. (Fuck.)

MURDO: Because everything's different from what I *expected*.

CHARLEY: Of course.

MURDO: And there are a number of uncleared up points.

CHARLEY: Because a boy of your calibre:

MURDO: Because I want *everything* to be cleared up.

CHARLEY: Mr Bybugger will be delighted.

Pause.

MURDO *goes to phone. Thinks better of it.*

MURDO: (Delighted?) Oh, ah *will he be delighted?*

CHARLEY: Delighted.

MURDO: Because Mr Dick thought he might be too busy to talk.

CHARLEY: Mr Dick? Mr *Dick*?

MURDO: Yes.

CHARLEY: Because Mr Dick's got it all wrong. Mr Bybugger would be delighted to talk to you *anytime*.

Pause.

MURDO *goes to phone.*

I mean I can understand you wanting to talk to Bobby.

MURDO *picks up phone.*

Because Bobby (he gets me to call him Bobby) Bobby's a brilliant bloke that speaks awful well of you.

MURDO: Oh, ah what does he *say*?

CHARLEY: I can understand you wanting to talk to him.

MURDO: I mean: what does he say about me?

CHARLEY: You'd obviously prefer to talk to him than to talk to me.

MURDO: Oh, ah/ (What?) No! I mean: 'yes'. I mean: I didn't know I *could* talk to you.

MURDO *puts phone down.*

CHARLEY: Well I want you to know you can tell me your problems any time you like. (Fuck.)

MURDO: Oh, ah thanks.

CHARLEY: That's all right.

MURDO: Is it all right?

CHARLEY: Oh (fuck) yes.

MURDO: Thanks.

Pause.

CHARLEY: But it's a bastarding pity, all the same.

MURDO: Pardon?

CHARLEY: A pity about the money.

MURDO: (Sorry.) What money?

CHARLEY: A pity there's no decent money to pay a talent like you a decent wage, a decent commission. (Fuck.) Take me: Not one sale, not one commission from a sale these two rotten months. Because see if I was your age, son, with a talent like yours on you? And. Don't think I *mean* anything by this. But if I was you I'd find myself alternative/

MURDO: Oh, ah Mr Hood. Thanks. But I don't mind if I don't do any sales. I mean: I don't need to do any sales.

CHARLEY: You don't mind?

MURDO: No.

CHARLEY: Because that's bastarding *big* of you.

MURDO: If that's all right.

CHARLEY: But don't let's talk jobbying *wet* around here. Because we're *all* in it for the money. (Or in some cases the nooky.)

MURDO: I'm not in it for the money . . .
Oh, ah would Mr Bybugger *mind*? Surely
he couldn't mind if I wanted to
concentrate on making Glasgow a wholly
healthy city . . . I mean: even if it meant
not doing any sales.

CHARLEY: You don't *mind* if you don't
do any . . . ?

MURDO: Sales . . . No!

CHARLEY: Oh? . . . And you want to
make Glasgow a . . . ?

MURDO: A wholly healthy city . . . Surely
he wouldn't mind.

CHARLEY: A wholly healthy Glasgow?

MURDO: Yes exactly, Mr Hood . . . I mean
surely he wouldn't mind if Glasgow was a
city of perfectly-proportioned, sinuous
but not over-developed physiques?
Surely he wouldn't mind if Glasgow was a
city of non-smoking, non-drinking
joggers? Surely he wouldn't mind if
Glasgow was a city of reposeful but alert
minds? Do you think he would mind?

CHARLEY: Mind? . . . Murdo my boy son.
Mr Bybugger will be delighted.
Congratulations. *I'm* delighted.

Shakes MURDO's hand.

Because the originality of the concept is
dazzling.

MURDO: I mean: I know it's a mammoth
task. Requiring a superhuman effort. I
can only hope I'm big enough. I mean: do
you think I'm big enough to achieve a
wholly healthy Glasgow by 1990?

CHARLEY: You're big enough. And
Murdo, son. If there's anything I can do
to help you, you know where I am. Aye, a
wholly healthy Glasgow, right enough.

MURDO: So, do you think Mr Bybugger
would mind if I didn't take my equal share
of the sales prospects?

CHARLEY: Oh no.

MURDO: Because if Mr Bybugger insisted
that I take my equal share I'd *have to* take
them (Sorry.)

CHARLEY: I promise you Mr Bybugger
won't mind you giving up your sales
prospects for a wholly healthy Glasgow.
He'll be delighted.

Pause.

MURDO: Oh, ah will I phone Mr Bybugger
up and tell him?

CHARLEY: 'Phone Bobby up and tell
him'. You could do. The other hand may
I make you a suggestion, Murdo?

MURDO: Oh, ah *yes*, Mr Hood.

CHARLEY: Imagine with me, Murdo, one
morning early in 1990, Mr Bybugger
emerges from the Empire Hotel on the
first morning of a visit to the Glasgow
branch. He emerges and he sees before
him a city of what was it?

MURDO: Perfectly-proportioned sinuous
physiques.

CHARLEY: Perfectly-proportioned
sinuous physiques. And what was it?

MURDO: Non-smoking, non-drinking
joggers.

CHARLEY: Non-smoking, non-drinking
joggers. And what was it?

MURDO: Reposeful but alert minds.

CHARLIE: Reposeful but alert minds.
Yes, imagine it. And imagine the joy
slowly appearing in Bobby Bybugger's
face. And imagine how much greater that
joy will be if it comes a *complete fucking
surprise*. (Employ your nut on this.) Then
he would walk in here and we would be
able to tell him that the wholly healthy
Glasgow operation has been directed by
you in the *gym* department and ably
assisted by me in the *sales* department.
(Am I right, am I wrong?)

MURDO: You're right Mr Hood . . . So can
I ask you about my problems now?

CHARLEY: Your problems? Oh fire away.
(Fuck.)

MURDO: I'll tell you them if you like.

CHARLEY: Because I'm all jobbying ears.

Pause.

MURDO: Well were you trying to renew
Mr Stein's membership on his first visit
today? (Contrary to Spartan Health
procedures.)

CHARLEY: No. Where did you get that
idea?

MURDO: And I'm sorry I didn't knock the
door for Donald.

CHARLEY: Eh? *What*?

MURDO: Because I'm sorry I didn't knock Donald Dick's door. (Will you have to tell Mr Bybugger?)

CHARLEY: We'll give that one a miss, Murdo son. Don't be fretting.

MURDO: I promise I won't do it again.

CHARLEY: Oh . . . *great*. Now. Where did you get the idea I was trying to renew Mr Stein's membership?

MURDO: I thought *you* said you tried to renew Mr Stein's membership?

CHARLEY: Haw heh: Craigie Stein was so impressed by you he enquired after a membership extension *himself*.

MURDO: I thought you said you tried, you *almost* renewed him.

CHARLEY: So Mr Stein was disappointed when I had to tell him the six visits rule.

Pause.

MURDO: And Donald said maybe/

CHARLEY: Donald?

MURDO: I mean Mr Dick. Mr Dick said you/

CHARLEY: Because oh ho now, Murdo son, Donald. Donald is a gorgeous person. Known the bastard years. And. Brilliant at the massaging job. Not a word against him. Except. An erratic cunt, a fly jobby you can't trust.

Pause.

MURDO: I wasn't to know Donald can't be trusted. (Sorry.)

CHARLEY: So watch what you say to Donald.

MURDO: Mr Bybugger didn't warn me.

CHARLEY: Because he's got none of our *talent*.

Pause.

MURDO: So why did Mr Bybugger *employ* Mr Dick? (Sorry.)

CHARLEY: Oh ho now, Murdo son gorgeous: because talent does not grow on pavements. And. You go out to work every day/ If you *choose* to go out to work every day you are *surrounded by a total dearth* of talent. *Oh* aye: a plethora of wankers: this world, this city. (I try to act normal.)

Pause.

MURDO: So Mr Dick must have *lied* to me, Mr Hood.

CHARLEY: A total liar, our Donny, unfortunately.

MURDO: I mean: *I see what you mean.*

CHARLEY: Misrepresenting me to fuck like that.

MURDO: Because Mr Dick told me you were *smoking* in here today. (Sorry.)

CHARLEY: Me?

MURDO: Smoking, *contrary to procedures*.

CHARLEY: So see what I mean about Donald?

MURDO: Oh, ah yes, Mr Hood. And is it true Mr Bybugger eats junk food when he's away from Pontefract?

Pause.

CHARLEY: Mr Bybugger? . . . What do you think about this yourself?

MURDO: I don't think he does.

CHARLEY: There's your answer. Who told you this garbage? No don't tell me:/

CHARLEY ⎱
MURDO ⎰   Donald.

Pause.

MURDO: So I don't know if I can work with Donald. Because someone who can't be trusted might try to stop us making Glasgow a wholly healthy/

CHARLEY: He keeps out our way, son. He stays in here, in his massage chambers, in his own *department*. So don't worry. Because not being able to trust Donald is *entirely irrelevant*.

MURDO: Oh . . . I see . . . Thanks .

CHARLEY: So is that you happy now?

MURDO: Oh, ah *yes*.

CHARLEY: Because you don't need to bother about Donald.

MURDO: I know Mr Hood. Because I can trust *you*. In fact, Mr Hood, I trust you *completely*.

CHARLEY: Of course you can. Oh aye. Aye. (Fuck.)

MURDO: And Donald is entirely irrelevant?

CHARLEY: Of course he is. Although. He is brilliant at the massage and as long as he sticks to his own department we/

MURDO: Massage?

CHARLEY: We/ Aye. Massage is Donald's department.

MURDO: What is the role of massage in the health of the body?

CHARLEY: Oh, Donny will tell you/

MURDO: Because massage wasn't included in the ten-day initiation training-course.

CHARLEY: Donny/

MURDO: Why *wasn't* it included if it has a role in the health of the /

CHARLEY: Donny/

MURDO: And if it doesn't have a role in the health of the body I'm not interested in it.

CHARLEY: It does have a role, Murdo son. Donny will tell you about it. In fact: let's set one up for you.

MURDO: Oh, ah/

CHARLEY: What am I saying? I've *already* set one up for you. Because see this special I was talking about? You'll never guess what it is? . . . A massage. (Ta ra.)

MURDO: I don't want a massage unless it *definitely* has a role in the health of the/

CHARLEY: When Donald gives you the massage you'll be so bastarding elated you won't need to ask questions. So is that you happy yet?

MURDO: Oh, ah yes.

CHARLEY: Good. So/

MURDO: Except.

CHARLEY: So/ Another problem, uh?)

MURDO: Why is the closed circuit not at reception, where it belongs?

CHARLEY: To / What

MURDO: And who's that in the gym?

MURDO *goes over to closed circuit monitor.*

CHARLEY: Nobody in the gym?

CHARLEY *follows him over.*

Oh for fuck's sake, it's big Rab. Big Rab McGuigan back early from Benidorm.

MURDO: Because there's no one in the gym to give Mr McGuigan some attention.

CHARLEY: No attention won't worry Rab. (Fuck.)

MURDO: So could I go and give him some attention?

CHARLEY: That won't worry Rab. (What?)

MURDO: Could I?

CHARLEY: Eh? Oh *aye.* Aye, off you go. (Fuck.)

MURDO: Oh, ah thanks. (Sorry.)

MURDO *goes out through gym.*

CHARLEY: Now. Where the fuck's Donny? 'I won't be long,' he goes. 'The Empire Hotel is a shitehole.' . . . Where the fuck's *Donny?* Where the fuck's *Alana?*

Pause.

CHARLEY *runs over to gym exit.*

CHARLEY (*shouts off*) Hey Murdo.

MURDO (off): Yes, Mr Hood

CHARLEY: So you first arrived the club, up reception, you see anyone standing chatting the Alana, the receptionist?

MURDO (*off*): Oh, ah I wasn't looking. (Sorry.)

CHARLEY: So you didn't see the punter, the Stein punter, the punter I took over from you?

MURDO (*off*): Not looking can be a fault of mine, I know.

CHARLEY: The punter with the limp.

MURDO: I think it might be because I'm so enthusiastic.

CHARLEY: I see. (*Quiet:*) Do I fuck. (*Loud:*) Thanks.

DONALD *comes in from reception.*

DONALD: Right, my shagpile's dry, give me a hand down with it . . . Where's Murdo? . . . Because is that Murdo beating it already? . . . So give me a hand down with my shagpile before the footballer comes . . . Come on.

CHARLEY: Where's Alana?

DONALD: I've got my atmosphere to think about. (Alana?)

CHARLEY: Alana.

DONALD: Alana's *nowhere* . . . Because she's *not* the bar, the Empire Hotel.

CHARLEY: Well thank fuck for that . . . You sure about this?

DONALD: I'm *sure*. (Fuck.) . . . So *is* this Murdo beating it yet?

Knocking.

Pause.

Knocking.

DONALD (*loud*): Come in.

MURDO *comes in from the gym.*

MURDO: Oh Mr Hood . . . Hello, Mr Dick. Mr Hood I meant to ask you something.

CHARLEY: Yes?

MURDO: It's because of my enthusiasm.

Pause.

CHARLEY: Yes, Murdo son?

Pause.

MURDO: Please may I work through my lunch hours?

Long pause.

Lights out.

ACT TWO

DONALD *and* CHARLEY *come in from reception, with* DONALD's *carpet, which* DONALD *arranges into place.*

CHARLEY (*entering*): But Donny boy, son. Your nooky will be *no* problem to Murdo . . . Because Murdo is the younger generation. And. So the younger generation have been brought up different. They are a bunch of broad-minded cunts you can't reason with.

DONALD: Just leave our arrangements *exactly as they are.*

CHARLEY: Murdo is a abnormal business opportunity.

DONALD: Why can't he just beat it?

CHARLEY: 18 years old and totally *not* into the acquisition of wealth yet.

DONALD: I practically had him beating it.

CHARLEY: Put your prejudice to one side, uh? (Use the bastard.)

DONALD: You've no right to *risk* my nooky.

CHARLEY: And. Because no cunt catches me out *not* taking advantage. (Risk?)

DONALD: Nooky's *my whole life.*

Pause.

CHARLEY: Risk your *nooky*? Because for fuck's sake, Donny. A big bold risk might just *maximise* your nooky. I mean: from tomorrow: the Glasgow boys come rolling in off the planes. Oh *aye*, man. And. Wanting to maintain the holiday physique, the holiday suntan, the holiday bastarding feeling. So we stick Murdo down the gym, happy crusading, happy keeping the members *ecstatic*. And. Meantime: I am sitting up reception *concentrating* lining you up every last possibility of nooky. So my plan enamours you?

DONALD: Your plan's garbage: so I am warning you and this backfires I go to London.

CHARLEY: You? You wouldn't go to London.

DONALD: I might just *go* to London.

CHARLEY: Fuck off to London then.

DONALD: I'll go to London *if and when I choose.*

Pause.

I mean: what if Murdo tells Bobby?

CHARLEY: Murdo *won't* tell Bobby.

DONALD: Because Murdo and Bobby are like that. (*Gestures.*) And Bobby is an anti-bent arsehole.

CHARLEY: I'll make sure he *doesn't tell* Bobby . . . So you *definitely* saw fuck all the bar, the Empire Hotel?

DONALD: Nothing.

CHARLEY: Good.

DONALD: Fuck all, as you say.

CHARLEY: Great. I mean: good to *know* that Alana Craigie are not *together.*

DONALD: The other hand I only managed a quick look up, look down the signing in sheet.

CHARLEY: That I am not a half-baked cunt after all. (Pardon?) . . . You had a quick what? On what what? So since when the bar, the Empire Hotel acquire a signing in sheet?

DONALD: Reception.

CHARLEY: Eh? Can a guy get to know what gives?

DONALD: Reception, the Empire Hotel.

CHARLEY: Reception, the Empire Hotel?

DONALD: Yes.

Pause.

CHARLEY: What for? You looked up, you looked down the signing in sheet reception, the Empire Hotel *what for?*

DONALD: I've to avoid the porter.

CHARLEY: The porter? Oh for fuck's sake, Donny. *What's going on?*

DONALD: Because it's more than my life's worth to *not* avoid the porter, the Empire Hotel. Did I not tell you about this, Charley? I could've *sworn* I told you about this. I meant to. (Sorry.) Well. Several weeks ago, right? I'm standing the bar, the Empire Hotel. This guy comes up to me. He comes up to me, he

goes, 'Follow me, uh?' So I follow him out the lobby. I'm out the lobby, he's standing the lift, the back, the lift, coming across the flagrant come on. I thought, 'Fuck'. (You know.) I goes in the lift, he shuts the door, we go up, he stops it. He stops it? He *jams* it between floors. He goes, 'Take your dick out.' I goes, 'Pardon?' He goes, 'Take your dick out and *come on.*' I goes, 'What?' He goes, 'You head.' I goes, 'OK.' So after the wee episode we come out the lift *past half the bastarding staff* the Empire Hotel waiting to *get in* the lift. And. Some wise cunt goes, 'Could you credit the depths this porter guy will stoop to? Because imagine going with *that.*' So 'that' Charley is *me.* I mean: *me*? I've had *coachloads* of porters after *me* in *my* time. (Fuck.) And you want to see the uncouth the youth to me *ever since.* So see this porter, the Empire Hotel, right? I'm avoiding him . . . Sorry but that's it.

CHARLEY: Is that *it.*

DONALD: Because that's *it.*

CHARLEY: Well ra ha ha, right enough, you kill me. And . . . And when's the date this episode?

DONALD: A few weeks ago there . . . Why do you/

CHARLEY: Because I thought you said you weren't going to be the bar, the Empire Hotel *long*?

DONALD: I wasn't long.

CHARLEY: You *were* long. (Long as fuck.)

DONALD: I wasn't long.

CHARLEY: Bastarding ages, you were.

DONALD: Was I? How long was I? Because I don't know how long I was. Do I?

Pause.

CHARLEY: Well ra ha ha. Aye ra ha ha you kill me. So that's you had your nooky?

DONALD: I have not/

CHARLEY: So you'll not be wanting it *again.*

DONALD: I have *not* had my nooky.

CHARLEY: You won't be wanting the footballer *now*.

DONALD: I *will* be wanting the footballer. I *had better get* the footballer. Because I have not had my nooky. And even if I had had my nooky who the bastarding hell do you think you are? The nooky police?

Pause.

DONALD *sits at closed circuit.*

I'm occupied.

CHARLEY: Aye ra ha ha and OK, Donny. I'll line you up the footballer as soon as he phones up. (Fuck.)

DONALD: I thought he was meeting the bird, the bar, the Empire Hotel.

CHARLEY: So did I. So I wish he'd *hurry up* and phone up.

Pause.

The Empire Hotel? The signing-in sheet? Haw heh here: how come you looked up, looked down the signing-in sheet *at all*? Because the Alana is *not* going to be hiring a room. Because the Alana's got a perfectly presentable two apartment.

DONALD: She might have wanted to shack up *in style* the professional footballer.

CHARLEY: So she wants to shack up in style she shacks up in my place.

DONALD: And I thought you wanted me to check on her.

CHARLEY: My place had an interior decorator. ((Me check on *her*?) Because I check on no cunt. I get her to check on *me*. (I only wanted to know she was OK.) So I did. So . . . I'm going the bar, the Empire Hotel.

DONALD: Oh are you?

CHARLEY: See you later.

DONALD: I'm occupied.

CHARLEY *goes to go.*

And who's that in the gym?

CHARLEY *stops, and goes to look.*

Because that looks like Murdo.

CHARLEY: It is Murdo. (What of it?)

Pause.

DONALD: So what's Murdo doing talking to big Rab?

CHARLEY: So Murdo wants to give Rab some attention.

DONALD: Because no one talks to big Rab McGuigan.

CHARLEY: So I says to him: 'OK' (Fuck.)

DONALD: And big Rab does not look happy.

CHARLEY: Big Rab looks bastarding miserable.

DONALD: Bastarding in torture

CHARLEY: Bastarding in agony.

DONALD: So big Rab is just about to/

CHARLEY: And oh for fuck's sake: big Rab is going to/

DONALD }
CHARLEY } Big Rab's lost his temper.

Pause.

CHARLEY: So ra ha ha. Aye ra ha ha. Because Murdo will have to learn to *not* give Rab attention. Otherwise Murdo will be no bastarding use to me.

CHARLEY *goes to go.*

DONALD: So what if the Alana, the Craigie phone up?

CHARLEY *stops.*

Heh. What if the Alana, the Craigie, the *Bobby* calls?

CHARLEY: The Alana, the Craigie get their number. I'll call them back. If it's Bobby go to him, 'Just hold on a minute.' Or, or no. Tell him to call back a wee minute, I'm in the lavvy. Or, or *definitely* no. You say I'm in the lavvy he'll go, 'Call him *out* the lavvy.' Say I'm in a sale. (Fuck.)

CHARLEY *goes to go. Stops himself.*

And the Murdo comes up here asking for me don't, for fuck's sake, tell the cunt where I am. He'll tell Bobby.

CHARLEY *goes to go, feeling for cigarettes. Remembers.*

So remember buy yourself cigarettes, Charley, uh?

DONALD: You're *not* smoking my massage chambers.

CHARLEY: Do yourself a favour.

CHARLEY *goes to go.*

DONALD: Because no more cigarettes my *newly-cleaned shagpile* . . . And there goes Murdo with a face.

CHARLEY *stops.*

And look *at* the face on Murdo.

CHARLEY *crosses, looks at the screen, laughs.* DONALD *joins him, Laughter builds and they take their attention off screen. Knocking.* CHARLEY *continues laughing.*

DONALD (*shouts*): Come in.

CHARLEY *stops laughing.*

MURDO *comes in from gym.*

CHARLEY *and* DONALD *look at him simultaneously, see his face and immediately start laughing again.* MURDO *holds himself above it, until they subside.*

MURDO: I'll have to leave here. . . Sorry . . . Well Mr McGuigan is doing a non-Spartan Health work-out.

CHARLEY: Hear that, Donny?

MURDO: He is taking rests *every ninety seconds.*

CHARLEY: Trust Rab McGuigan to go do a non-Spartan Health work-out.

MURDO: And he said that no one had ever *tried* to *remotivate* him.

DONALD: So is this you definitely leaving?

CHARLEY: *Remotivate* him? (Shut up, Donny.)

DONALD: I was just getting to know and love you too.

CHARLEY: (Donny!)

MURDO: And he said that he didn't want *anyone* to ever try remotivating him *again* . . . So he's *continuing* with his non-Spartan Health work-out.

CHARLEY: Don't leave because of Rab, son. (Fuck.)

MURDO: *Even though* a non-Spartan Health work-out might *ruin his whole life.*

CHARLEY: Rab *always was* a problem.

MURDO: Then he *swore* at me. So I'll have

to definitely leave here.

Pause.

CHARLEY: A fucking bastard that Rab McGuigan. Imagine *swearing* at Murdo. But, as I say, son. Don't leave because of Rab McGuigan.

MURDO: I'll *have to.* Because I want everything in my gym department to go perfectly.

DONALD: Of for fuck's sake: 'perfectly'.

CHARLEY: (Donny!) *So* Murdo, son: you *prefer* the Spartan Health system?

MURDO: It's the *only* system.

CHARLEY: I know Mr Bybugger recommends it for members.

MURDO: It's the *company* system.

CHARLEY: And the Bobby tell you how to enforce it?

MURDO: Oh, ah but if members are instructed correctly from the beginning.

CHARLEY: Some these guys have been working out since long before Spartan Health work-outs were invented.

MURDO: Older members must be *re*motivated.

CHARLEY: So how you get on with remotivating big Rab McGuigan down there?

MURDO: I wasn't to know no previous remotivational work had taken place with Mr McGuigan. (Had it?)

CHARLEY: Because when I think the times I've went down my hands, my knees *tried* to remotivate big Rab.

MURDO: How can a man get genuinely fit *unless* he does a Spartan Health work-out? Because a rest *every ninety seconds* could be fatal, Mr Hood.

Pause.

CHARLEY: So Murdo. With the calibre we've got on us you know and I know it's brilliant being fit as fuck. (Take me: I jog myself to buggery.) But a low calibre twat like Rab McGuigan cannot tell the difference between a remotivation and his wee Aunty Renee. Because all Rab wants is a waistline, a pair of shoulders and a giant prick. Get a grip, Murdo, uh? The guy's not all right the head. So I strolls in the gym one day, the Rab's wanking himself off. I goes to him: 'What the fuck do you think you're doing?' He goes, 'I'm doing my prick presses Charley.' I goes, 'Get to fuck you dirty cunt you.' He goes, 'My prick presses are brilliant, Charley. Fifty repetitions and you can add four inches a work-out.' . . . So, Murdo, I was just saying to Donny how it's really great the way you were tolerating Rab down there, how I really *admired* you, you know?

MURDO: Oh, ah you *admired* me?

CHARLEY: So it's a shock to learn you are one the most intolerant cunts going.

MURDO: Oh/

CHARLEY: And I thought you were a guy with calibre could put up with a harmless half-normal ballhead doing a non-company work-out quietly the corner the gym. Yes, I admired you. However, hold on a wee minute I do an errand before you say goodbye.

MURDO: Oh ah/

CHARLEY: In fact, Murdo gorgeous, hold on get *your massage* before you go.

MURDO: Oh, ah/

DONALD: His *massage*?

CHARLEY: Because I don't bear grudges.

DONALD: Who's providing the massage?

MURDO: I could try again to remotivate Mr McGuigan. Because it was my enthusiasm which made me tolerate Mr McGuigan so long.

CHARLEY: I know: you enthusiastic cunt you.

DONALD: *The massage*!

Pause.

CHARLEY: Massage? Haw heh Murdo: that's *your* massage the Donny is referring to. And. A brilliant sense of humour, our Donny. 'Who's providing the massage?' Aye ra ha ha: who else but Donald – the touch – Dick.

DONALD: (And is he fuck.)

CHARLEY: So you will wait till I get back, Murdo son?

MURDO: Oh, ah/

CHARLEY: (Keep your gob *shut*, Donny.)

MURDO: Oh, ah/

CHARLEY: You will wait avail yourself the massage, Murdo, before you leave?

MURDO: Oh, ah/

CHARLEY: Because see you guys in a minute.

CHARLIE *goes out to reception.*

MURDO: (I might *not* leave.)

Pause.

Thank you very much for giving me a massage, Mr Dick.

DONALD: Don't thank me.

MURDO: I'm very grateful.

DONALD: Because you're not fucking getting a massage.

Pause.

MURDO: Oh *why*? (Sorry.)

DONALD: You just aren't.

MURDO: Don't you want to give me a massage?

DONALD: No. I'm a miserable hard-hearted bastard.

Pause.

MURDO: I wouldn't mind paying.

DONALD: Get to fuck.

MURDO: I mean: if I'm not *entitled to* a free Spartan Health massage, I'll pay.

DONALD: I don't *want* to give you a massage, OK?

Pause.

MURDO: OK.

Long pause.

DONALD: What's going on?

MURDO: Oh, ah nothing.

DONALD: So why don't you speak?

MURDO: Sorry. I'll try not to not speak in future.

Long pause.

DONALD: Oh, for fuck's sake: away home Murdo, uh?

MURDO: Oh, ah do you *want* me to go

home? (I *don't want* to go home. Sorry.)

DONALD: Because, *as Charley says*, you're an obnoxious intolerant cunt.

MURDO: Oh but I'm not ever going to be intolerant again. Am I?

Pause.

DONALD: What is it with you? Ten days with Bobby Bybugger in Pontefract, you don't want to go straight home. Why?

MURDO: I don't like going home . . . I come from a problem background.

DONALD: Get to fuck.

MURDO: *It is.* (Sorry.)

DONALD: In what way?

MURDO: I prefer to not talk about it.

DONALD: Your background can't be as big a problem as mine.

MURDO: I don't like going home to my parents. (Sorry.)

DONALD: You ungrateful shite you. I haven't even got a background. I haven't even got a set of parents to *go home to.*

MURDO: Oh but, Mr Dick.

DONALD: Yes?

MURDO: You don't know what it's like . . . You see my father was asked to leave the police force for drinking on duty. So he lies in bed now, *all day.* And my mother is a *very fat woman.* She gets out of breath just *climbing down the steps* to the back garden. And my sister works in a hamburger restaurant and she *eats the food.*

DONALD: I see what you mean/

MURDO: So what would Mr Bybugger say if he found out?

DONALD: A bastarding disaster area your background. (Mr Bybugger?)

Telephone. DONALD *picks it up, listens and impulsively hands it over to* MURDO.

Ask him yourself.

MURDO (*to phone*): Oh, ah, Murdo Caldwell here, Mr Bybugger.

DONALD: But don't mention/

MURDO: Sorry, Mr Bybugger.

DONALD: Don't mention Charley Hood.

MURDO: Oh, ah yes. 'Spartan Health. May we help you?' in future. (*To* DONALD:) What?

DONALD: Don't say Charley's gone out.

MURDO: Oh, ah/

DONALD: Because Bobby knows he's already had his half-hour break. So/

MURDO: Oh, ah/

DONALD: Just don't say Charley's gone out.

MURDO: Charley Hood's in the gym.

DONALD: And don't say he's in the gym. (Oh no.)

MURDO: I can see Charley Hood on the closed circuit screen.

DONALD: And can you fuck.

MURDO: I just happen to be standing by it . . . At reception, yes.

DONALD: Reception? (For fuck's sake.)

MURDO: Yes, Mr Bybugger. I will.

MURDO *puts phone down.*

DONALD: So sorry I shoved the phone in your face. I'm a hasty cunt.

MURDO: No. I should have been *prepared* to answer with the Spartan Health telephone procedure.

DONALD: You're right. I thought it would be a brilliant test for Spartan Health telephone procedure. You failed.

Pause.

MURDO: And the closed circuit *should be* at reception. I mean: what would Mr Bybugger think if he knew I was standing beside it in the *massage chambers*?

DONALD: I don't know.

MURDO: I'm taking it back to reception.

DONALD: Take it where the fuck you like.

MURDO: Back to reception after Mr Bybugger phones back.

DONALD: Because I don't/ *Phoning back*?

MURDO: (Sorry.)

DONALD: What's Bobby phoning back for?

MURDO: To talk to Mr Hood.

DONALD: Oh *no.*

MURDO: Where *is* Mr Hood?

DONALD: You should have said Charley was in a sale.

MURDO: Where is he?

DONALD: A sale's the only bastard Bobby won't ask us to interrupt. (What?) Oh *I* don't know. (Fuck.)

Pause.

MURDO: If Mr Hood doesn't come back in time what will happen to him?

DONALD: Nothing will happen to *Charley Hood. You* covered up for *him.*

MURDO: You said, 'Don't say he's gone out.'

DONALD: You said he's in the gym . . . I mean, for fuck's sake, *why* the gym?

MURDO: Because oh, ah I *don't know why.*

Pause.

DONALD: So Charley said he'll not be long.

MURDO: I didn't know he *wasn't* in the gym.

DONALD: Sometimes . . . Charley *does do* what he says he'll do.

MURDO: So what will happen to *me?*

Pause.

Telephone rings.

DONALD: Fuck it, son. You'll *survive.* Look at me.

MURDO *picks up telephone.*

MURDO (*on phone*): Oh, ah Spartan Health. *May we help you?*

Pause.

No, Mr Bybugger.

Pause.

Mr Hood *wasn't* in the gym, Mr Bybugger.

Pause.

I *don't know* where he is, Mr Bybugger.

Pause.

Sorry, Mr Bybugger. I will always tell the truth in future, Mr Bybugger . . . Bye, Mr Bybugger.

MURDO *puts telephone down.*

(*To* DONALD:) Will Charley Hood *also* be in receipt of a reprimand?

DONALD: Don't bother about Bobby Bybugger.

MURDO: Because that's *twice* I've been told off.

DONALD: Bobby is not all right in the head.

MURDO: Twice I've been *shouted at.*

DONALD: Why else eat all that organic wank?

MURDO: I didn't know Mr Bybugger *shouted.* (Pardon?)

DONALD: Why else go about a daft big muscled cunt?

Pause.

MURDO: But Mr Bybugger was right to tell me off.

DONALD: So don't worry about Bobby.

MURDO: I should have been prepared with the telephone *procedure.* I should have told Mr Bybugger nothing but the truth.

DONALD: He gets a kick out of *taking advantage.*

MURDO: So I will always tell the truth in future. (What?)

DONALD: Bobby's a bastard.

Pause.

MURDO: It doesn't matter what you say about Mr Bybugger, Mr Dick. I know I can't trust you. (Sorry.)

DONALD: Pardon?

MURDO: Oh, but don't worry because I know you're not all that relevant.

DONALD: What?

MURDO: Mr Hood told me you're not all that relevant.

DONALD: Not *relevant?*

MURDO: So it *doesn't matter* if Mr Hood and I can't trust you.

DONALD: Charley Hood. (I might have known.) The lying two-sided cunt.

Pause.

So this means you trust Charley Hood?

MURDO: Oh, ah yes. Completely.

DONALD: You trust *Charley Hood*? And *completely* too? (Fuck.) Don't make me piss myself. Because when I think of the jobbying connivances I've taken from him over the years, till I'm about demented. I mean: earlier the night, an example, he lies his bastarding nut off get me get Alana out the way the Stein punter. I've told Charley, 'Give your birds peace, uh?' But, *no*. And all this for Alana. Alana, the prick in the red frock, reception. Oh but Alana: she and I go *right* back, by the way. We slag each other off on a regular basis. Talk about laugh. So she tells me the lot. Her nooky, *everything*. Where, how, who. *Who*? For fuck's sake: the porter, the Empire Hotel, Rab McGuigan, Bobby Bybugger. Don't tell Charley. Even Bobby Bybugger exploited her in Pontefract. Her on the initiation training-course, so she was. Oh aye. Alana's lifestyle's fabulous. Charley Hood tells you not to trust me? (I mean: *me*!) I am one the most put upon cunts going. So come on to fuck, Murdo, son.

MURDO: I thought there was *something* wrong with Charley Hood. Because he let me off/

DONALD: *Something*?

MURDO: He let me off lightly when I told him I didn't knock your door.

DONALD: Eh?

MURDO: I don't like a lack of thoroughness like that.

DONALD: Of course you don't.

MURDO: A knocking doors rule ought to be adhered to.

DONALD: Exactly. (Fuck.)

Pause.

MURDO: And may I ask a question?

DONALD: Oh God, aye.

MURDO: What is the role of massage in the health of the body?

DONALD: Massage?

MURDO: Massage!

DONALD: Absolutely sweet fuck all.

MURDO: I see.

DONALD: Useless for the body, massage.

MURDO: I thought so.

DONALD: Useless (*Pure* useless.)

MURDO: Because Mr Hood told me it had an *important* role in the health of the body. And that you would tell me about it.

DONALD: Not at all.

MURDO: It all makes sense now.

DONALD: Good. Glad for you.

MURDO: Because if massage had an important role in the health of the body Mr Bybugger would have *definitely* included it in the initiation training-course. Wouldn't he?

DONALD: So see what I mean?

MURDO: I see what you mean.

Pause.

But I don't think Mr Bybugger exploited Alana in Pontefract.

DONALD: Aye, he did. Because some cheeky boss pricks go too far.

MURDO: How do you know *Alana* didn't want to/ to experiment sexually with Mr Bybugger?

DONALD: The exploitation was unadulterated.

MURDO: Mr Bybugger is a genuine human being so I wouldn't be surprised if *Alana* had wanted to experiment with *him*. He is very forward-looking.

DONALD: Is he fuck.

MURDO: Very broad-minded and openly bisexual.

DONALD: And is he *definitely* fuck. Because Bybugger does not entertain bent goings on.

MURDO: Oh, ah that's not true.

DONALD: A deplorable attitude in the eighties . . . I mean: take, an instance, two guys meet the club. Two guys take a justifiable nooky interest each other. Because two guys with fuck all place else to go. Bobby would not approve them using Spartan Health Club for a sexual experiment. (Fuck.)

MURDO: I *agree* with the no-sex-on-the-premises rule.

DONALD: The/

MURDO: Because unchecked sex-on-the-premises would tend to *discourage* new members from joining and existing members from renewing.

DONALD: Who's going to enforce a no-nooky rule a building this size?

MURDO *picks up closed circuit monitor.*

MURDO: Someone will have to *try* to enforce it.

MURDO *makes to go out via reception.*

DONALD: So you know you said you were beating it?

MURDO *stops.*

I'd beat it if I was you.

MURDO *continues.*

MURDO *stops himself.*

MURDO: But what do you think of the no-sex-on-the-premises rule, Mr Dick?

DONALD: Yes?

MURDO: Don't you mind me taking the closed circuit monitor back? . . . Because if *I* leave here, who will be left to enforce it? . . . And Mr Dick?

DONALD: No.

MURDO: Back to reception?

DONALD: No.

MURDO: Back to *where it belongs*?

DONALD: Because *definitely* no.

MURDO *continues.*

MURDO *stops himself.*

MURDO: Do you think I could tolerate *not trusting anyone*? . . . I mean: is it *relevant* that I also don't trust Charley Hood?

CHARLEY *comes in from reception.*

DONALD: Bobby phoned.

CHARLEY: And?

DONALD: Murdo covered for you.

CHARLEY: Murdo cov/?

DONALD: But then Bobby phoned back.

CHARLEY: Covered for *me*? What?

DONALD: And found out Murdo was lying.

Pause.

CHARLEY: Thanks, son.

MURDO: Don't thank me.

CHARLEY: And don't worry about Bobby.

MURDO: I won't.

CHARLEY: Because I'll look after Bobby for you.

MURDO: Oh, don't say anything to Mr Bybugger.

CHARLEY: I'll put in a helpful word.

MURDO: Please.

CHARLEY: The least I can do. (Fuck.)

MURDO: Don't! . . . Because I didn't *intend* to help you. If you shouldn't've been out I wouldn't've helped you if I'd *known* you shouldn't've been out. I was confused. (Sorry.)

MURDO *goes out to reception with closed circuit monitor.*

CHARLEY: So Donny: guess who's the Empire Hotel, uh? . . . No *wait* a wee minute. (*Shouts off to reception*:) Heh Murdo: Where you going?

MURDO (*off*) I'm returning the monitor to reception.

CHARLEY (*to* DONALD): Thank fuck for that.

MURDO (*off*): Where it belongs.

CHARLEY (*shouts off*): Back down here right after, uh? Because we're doing you the massage the now.

MURDO (*off*): Oh, ah *now*? (Why?)

CHARLEY (*shouts off*): The now and *come on.*

MURDO (*off*): But Donald doesn't want to give me one.

CHARLEY: Fuck you said, Donny?

CHARLEY *fumbles for cigarettes. Remembers.*

(Because *fuck*.) (*Shouts off:*) Aye he *does.*

MURDO: He said he didn't.

CHARLEY (*shouts off*): So get ready, uh? (What?)

MURDO: You don't Mr Dick, do you?

DONALD *shakes his head.*

DONALD: No, I do not/

CHARLEY *covers* DONALD's *mouth.*

CHARLEY (*shouting off, improvising* DONALD's *voice*): I was only pulling your leg earlier, Murdo son. I'd love to give you a massage. Be gorgeous.

MURDO (*off*): Oh, ah no thanks. (*Further away*:) Because massage does not have an important role in the health of the body.

CHARLEY (*quiet*): Fuck that.

MURDO (*off*): Thanks. (*Gone.*)

CHARLEY *releases* DONALD.

DONALD: And if you think I was wasting my time, my labour giving Murdo one of my good massages, when he *definitely* won't accept my nooky-on-the-premises/

CHARLEY: He *won't*? Because how come you *know* he won't? . . . I told you *not to* bring it up. I mean do your jobbying *calculations*, Donny. The massage's *the lever* we're using *get him accept* your nooky.

Pause.

DONALD: So who was at the Empire Hotel?

CHARLEY: The Empire Hotel, Donny? Well, for starters, *not* the Alana, *not* the Craigie. But Donny, boy son: I took my time, looked up, looked down the signing in sheet . . . and found: *Bobby Bybugger*'s signature. (Ta ra.) . . . So Donny: come the morrow Bobby will *definitely* walk in here. So. That's you *definitely* giving Murdo a massage.

DONALD: Am I fuck.

CHARLEY: Because you don't give Murdo a massage – a high quality massage – I report your nooky to Bobby the morrow morning.

DONALD: And that will be right. So Bobby boots me and who takes my place?

CHARLEY: Murdo.

Pause.

DONALD: Murdo might leave.

CHARLEY: Murdo does not intend to leave. (I am not a fuckwit.)

DONALD: Murdo can't massage.

CHARLEY: Murdo can learn massage. (Because fuck all to it.)

DONALD: You heard Murdo say he's not interested in massage.

CHARLEY: He's not interested because whatever fucking garbage you said to him. And. He *will be* interested by the time *I've* finished with him.

DONALD: Murdo won't accept you raking in all the cash.

CHARLEY: Murdo *has* accepted it . . . Because Murdo trusts me completely.

Pause.

DONALD: You couldn't operate without me.

CHARLEY: Who couldn't?

DONALD: I will not be degraded by your vicious low-down blackmail.

CHARLEY: Because it is time to expand, Donny. So expand your vision, uh? An instructor the gym expands my money, expands your nooky, expands our operation.

DONALD: I will not be bribed while you run me down behind my back. Massage a cunt's been told a pair of disgusting lies about me.

CHARLEY: What the fuck's Murdo said next?

DONALD: My dignity in tatters.

CHARLEY: Because Murdo will have to learn to *not* talk behind our backs about *us* talking behind our backs. And Donny: get a grip, for fuck's sake. I run you down, you run me down: it's all in a day's labour.

DONALD: I'm the sensitive type. (At times.)

CHARLEY: I mean: so we boot each other the balls it's *OK*. It's for the long term *communal* gain, isn't it? And, as I say, Donny, expand your vision or you will wind up a totally non-viable entity.

DONALD: I want my nooky.

CHARLEY: OK. And I want my renewal.

DONALD: And I am not doing this

massage unless you *guarantee* me my nooky.

CHARLEY: So you're not big enough take a risk, uh?

DONALD: A guarantee, *I says*.

Telephone.

CHARLEY: Aye ra ha, you kill me.

CHARLEY *picks up telephone.*

'Guarantee me my nooky.' . . . (*To* *phone*:) Spartan Health. May we help you? . . . (*To* DONALD:) It's the voice of . . . your nooky. (*To phone*:) Hello there, Mr Stein . . . (*To* DONALD:) You nooky *guaranteed*. (To phone:) Where? Who? . . . Yes, because *oh* yes, Mr Stein . . . In fact, I'll check for you.

CHARLEY *holds up two fingers to* DONNY.

(*Loudly to* DONNY:) How many these early-cheap-rate renewals we got left, Mr Dick?

Holds phone towards DONALD.

DONALD (*very loud*):Two, Mr Hood.

CHARLEY *shakes his head.*

CHARLEY (*loud*): And will head office allow us to hold any of them for Mr Stein here till the morning, Mr Dick?

DONALD (*very loud*): I'm afraid not, Mr Hood.

CHARLEY (*very loud*): And how soon are they likely to be sold, Mr Dick

DONALD (*loud*): Oh, ah/

CHARLEY *holds two fingers very close.*

They could go anytime, Mr Hood.

CHARLEY (*to* DONALD): Thank you, Mr Dick. (*To phone*:) Did you hear that, Mr Stein? . . . See you in twenty minutes, Mr Stein.

CHARLEY *puts phone down.*

Pause.

So Donny: that's your nooky guaranteed *definitely.*

Pause.

DONALD: Right. Twenty minutes high-quality massage. Not a second more. Because massaging a miniature vomit like

Murdo is only going to make me realise how much I *want* my nooky.

CHARLEY: Aye ra ha ha, all that shite. So Donny: the Stein punter *does* meet the wee bird, the Empire Hotel. But she wants to go a curry. They *leave* the Empire Hotel. A taxi across town some curry-house she fancied. They sit down. They order. She goes the lavvy. Several minutes pass. She does not come back the lavvy. Half an hour passes. He realises he has had the boot in a big way. The boot in a big way? the *anti-climax* in a big way. So he is paying the bill, he is taxiing back here. Alone. So Donny. After the high-quality massage, we get Murdo brought round on nooky, I will line you up the footbaler. (Not that you deserve it: you obstacle-manufacturing cunt you.)

CHARLEY *feels for cigarettes.* *Remembers.*

(*Fuck.*)

Pause.

I'll go out buy a packet of cigarettes, uh Donny?

DONALD: *No!*

Pause.

CHARLEY: You're right. I'll get Murdo down. Because aye: I'll just have to get through this shiting awful massage somehow.

CHARLEY *goes to phone.*

DONALD: You're not smoking here.

CHARLEY: Because I go back out/

DONALD: You're not smoking here, flicking my shagpile, I've got a line up coming.

CHARLEY: I go back out/

DONALD: I've got my atmosphere to think about.

CHARLEY: Because *I go back out* (fuck) meanwhile Murdo strolls in you try the hand that's us well fucked.

CHARLEY *picks up phone.*

DONALD: You have *got to be* joking. Nooky with Murdo? I'd go, 'Have you come yet?' He'd go, 'Oh, ah I didn't know I *could* come. I haven't asked Mr Bybugger's permission.'

CHARLEY *listens to phone and suddenly puts it down.*

CHARLEY: So you say.

DONALD: I am not a child molester.

CHARLEY: So you say.

DONALD: A Sunday School teacher.

CHARLEY: Because so you say. (That's funny.)

DONALD: My taste is not in my arse.

Pause.

What's funny?

CHARLEY: Murdo was on the line.

Pause.

DONALD: Who to?

CHARLEY: I didn't want to listen in. *Did I?*

DONALD: Why the fuck not, for fuck's sake?

CHARLEY: Because I am not a nosey demoralizing bag of crumpled shite like you, am I?

DONALD *picks up telephone, listens and puts it down.*

DONALD: Murdo's off the line.

CHARLEY: Murdo was on the line.

DONALD: He's off the line *now*.

CHARLEY *picks it up, listens and puts it down.*

CHARLEY: So what was he *doing* on the line?

DONALD: I don't know. (Fuck.)

CHARLEY: Because what did you say made him *want* to go on the line?

DONALD: Nothing. Not a thing.

Pause.

CHARLEY ⎫
DONALD ⎭ So where the fuck *is* he?

Pause.

CHARLEY: I'm going to look.

DONALD: Because I don't know where he is.

CHARLEY *goes to go.*

And because I don't want Murdo wandering about/

Telephone.

Wandering about *fuck alone knows where.*

DONALD *picks up phone, listens, quickly passes it over to* CHARLEY.

CHARLEY (*to phone*): Spartan Health. May we help you?

DONALD: So *I'll* find Murdo. (Fuck.)

DONALD *goes out to reception.*

CHARLEY (*to phone*): Well hello *again*, Mr Stein.

DONALD (*off*): And you had better line me him up.

CHARLEY: (*You'll* be lucky you get a boot up the arse.) So Mr Stein, where/? . . . You're *still* at the curry house? . . . You trouble getting a taxi, I suppose? . . . Oh, so the wee bird turned up? (Fuck.) Uh? I mean you were just about to leave . . . you heard a scream, she was locked the lavvy . . . What a comical sound that must have/ . . . Aye ra ha ha, and I can just picture it . . . (Fuck.) . . . So that you on your way round here now, uh? . . . Oh the wee bird want to go a bevvy the bar, the Empire Hotel first?

DONALD *comes in from reception, 'in haste', unseen by* CHARLEY.

So after your wee drink, Mr Stein, you may be like pop over? I believe we do still have *one* early-cheap-rate renewal remaining . . . Oh, ah bye, Mr Stein.

We understand that MR STEIN *has hung up.*

DONALD: 'Bye, Mr Stein.'

CHARLEY *drops the phone violently on to the receiver.*

CHARLEY: Oh mammy, daddy, Donny don't/

DONALD: That you lost me my footballer again?

CHARLEY: Don't *do* that.

DONALD: Because no footballer/

CHARLEY ⎫
DONALD ⎭ No massage.

CHARLEY: I know. And. OK, Donny. No bastarding massage. Because do you think I can't get Murdo brought round *without* a massage? Because I can do any bastarding thing I choose with Murdo. So watch me go.

DONALD: You'll need to find him first.

CHARLEY: Watch me go *definitely*. (What?)

DONALD: You'll need to find Murdo, *I says*.

Pause.

CHARLEY: So where is he?

DONALD: Why don't we just boot him?

CHARLEY: Where is Murdo and *come on*?

DONALD: I almost had him booted at one point.

CHARLEY: Murdo is *not* getting booted.

DONALD: Because he is one of the most unpredictable pricks I've encountered.

Pause.

CHARLEY: So he's not reception?

DONALD: Not at reception? He's not *the* building.

CHARLEY: He's not the gym?

DONALD: I checked him the closed circuit.

CHARLEY: He's not the lavvy?

DONALD: He's not the lavvy.

CHARLEY: How do you know he's not the lavvy?

DONALD: He's not the lavvy!

CHARLEY: Because the closed circuit does not *show* the lavvy. (Thank fuck.)

DONALD: He's not the lavvy, because let's face it about Murdo: Murdo does not *go* the lavvy.

Pause.

CHARLEY: Uh? Oh *aye*. Aye ra ha ha, you kill me. OK, where *is* Murdo?

DONALD: I don't/

Knocking.

Pause.

CHARLEY: You going to do the massage?

DONALD: Am I fuck.

CHARLEY: OK. So I'll get him brought round without your pathetic useless massage and you can keep your gob shut, OK?

Knocking.

OK?

DONALD: I think I'll just go to London.

CHARLEY: Aye, go to London, for fuck's sake. (*Loud:*) Come in. (*Quiet:*) Go to London, give us all peace.

MURDO *comes in from reception.*

Pause.

Murdo gorgeous/

DONALD: Where have you been?

CHARLEY: (We were just wondering.)

MURDO: The Empire Hotel.

CHARLEY: Oh, the Empire Hotel?

DONALD: What the fuck for?

MURDO: I was looking for Mr Bybugger. (Sorry.)

Pause.

DONALD: How did you know he was at the Empire Hotel?

CHARLEY: Did you find him?

MURDO: I phoned up Pontefract and they told me.

CHARLEY: Did you find him?

DONALD: You'd no fucking right to phone up Pontefract.

MURDO: Yes, I found him.

CHARLEY: You did, uh? (Fuck.) So what did you say to him?

MURDO: Nothing.

DONALD: I might've wanted to phone up Pontefract and not been able to. (Nothing?)

CHARLEY: You said *nothing*?

MURDO: Mr Bybugger wouldn't *let me* say anything.

Pause.

CHARLEY *and* DONALD *laugh*

*simultaneously, and in spasmodic burst
thereafter through* MURDO's *speech.*

And Mr Bybugger was eating a sausage. I
don't mind if you two eat a sausage,
because I know I can't trust *you two*. But
if Mr Bybugger's eating a sausage who
can I trust? And then he told me off for
drinking on duty, when I wasn't drinking
on duty. I was only going to look for Mr
Bybugger to find out if it was *all right* not
to trust you two.

CHARLEY: You definitely said nothing?

MURDO: I didn't get a chance to. I didn't
know Mr Bybugger was such an angry
person. That's *three times* he's been angry
with me. Yes, he told me off for drinking
on duty and sent me back here.

DONALD: You're not on duty but.

MURDO: Oh, ah Mr Bybugger was quite
right:/

DONALD: And you *weren't* drinking.

MURDO: I volunteered to work. And I
placed myself in incriminating
circumstances just being *in* the bar, the
Empire Hotel.

DONALD: So I'd just beat it if I was you.

MURDO: So I don't know what I'm going
to do. (Pardon?)

DONALD: You might as well beat it.

MURDO: Oh, I can't do that.

DONALD: Why not?

MURDO: If I left what about a wholly
healthy Glasgow?

CHARLEY: Exactly.

Pause.

DONALD: What is this?

MURDO: Oh yes, Mr Dick. A wholly
healthy Glasgow by 1990.

DONALD: What's going on?

CHARLEY: And I'm helping you, Murdo
son, aren't I?

DONALD: Don't talk shite.

CHARLEY: Whether you like it or not
Donald a wholly healthy Glasgow by
1990. That right, Murdo?

MURDO: That's right, Mr Hood. (If
possible.)

Pause.

DONALD: Bobby won't like a wholly
healthy Glasgow.

CHARLEY: Bobby will be delighted.
Won't he son?

MURDO: Yes. And we're keeping it as a
surprise for him.

CHARLEY: And you won't get in our way,
Donny, will you?

MURDO: Oh, ah how could Mr Dick get in
our way if he sticks to his own
department?

DONALD: I won't be getting in your way.
(Fuck.) I might go to London.

CHARLEY: Exactly, son: he'll stick to his
own department. or even better: he'll
fuck off to London.

DONALD: But I'd leave if I was you,
Murdo.

MURDO: Oh, ah why?

CHARLEY: Pay no attention, son. In fact:
let's get to fuck out of here, out the cunt's
department . . . You coming?

MURDO: Why should I leave, Mr Dick?

DONALD: Because . . ./

CHARLEY: Donny!

DONALD: Because I'm bent.

CHARLEY: (Oh for *fuck's* sake.)

DONALD: Bent as fuck.

CHARLEY: Don't listen to him.

MURDO: Oh, I don't mind, Mr Dick.

CHARLEY: Don't pay/ (What?)

MURDO: I don't mind if you are a
homosexual, Mr Dick. I quite like you.

DONALD: That's bastarding unfortunate,
Murdo. Because, quite frankly, *you* give
me the vomit.

Pause.

CHARLEY: Aye ra ha ha, right enough,
you kill me Donny. So Murdo, I can see
this tolerance is a massive part of you.

MURDO: Oh yes, I'm very tolerant now,
Mr Hood, thanks to you.

CHARLEY: Of course you are. Your
tolerance is prominent.

DONALD: And not only am I bent, Murdo:/

CHARLEY: (Donny!) Your tolerance is/

DONALD: I'm bent on the premises.

Pause.

CHARLEY: So, as I was saying, Murdo son, if you are genuinely intent on getting a wholly healthy Glasgow you will encounter a lot of the flying wank of life on the journey, so you will. And./

MURDO: Is this true, Mr Dick?

DONALD: True as fuck.

CHARLEY: Who can say if it's true?

DONALD: Because see me: I am one the lowest quality cunts the world. Because there is not one guy going I haven't had my hand well down his trousers. (On the premises.)

Pause.

CHARLEY: Fascinating thing is, Murdo, I have never yet *seen* one these disgusting acts Donny says he commits.

MURDO: Mr Dick is either breaking the rules or he isn't. *Which*?

DONALD: I am.

CHARLEY: He isn't.

MURDO: Well I don't trust either of you. So I don't know who to believe.

DONALD: So I'd leave if I was you.

MURDO: If it's true I'll have to leave . . . Mr Hood?

CHARLEY: Yes, Murdo son?

MURDO: Why would Mr Dick lie about this?

CHARLEY: Oh, Murdo some these more frustrateder benders, they'll say anything impress you. 'Oh aye, Charley,' goes Donny, 'I've just done such and such so and so's body while he wasn't looking.' Not pleasant, is it? But my advice to you is: take pity, thank fuck you're not like that, OK? However you obviously don't want a wholly healthy Glasgow badly enough.

MURDO: I do.

CHARLEY: You don't *enough*.

DONALD: Aye. You don't enough. (Fuck.) You'd better go.

Pause.

MURDO: OK. I'll go.

Pause.

CHARLEY: A pity, all the same, you couldn't tolerate a few Donny's indiscreetnesses, even if he *does* do them.

DONALD: I do do them.

CHARLEY: Even if he does do them. A pity a really great *end* like a wholly healthy Glasgow should get fucked because you, sir, rate yourself well above the admittedly disgusting *means*.

MURDO: But if Mr Dick has sex-on-the-premises new members will be discouraged from/

DONALD: Exactly.

CHARLEY: Not at all.

MURDO: And existing members from/

DONALD: Exactly, *I said*.

MURDO: Existing members from/

CHARLEY: Murdo?

MURDO: Yes.

CHARLEY: May I say something here?

MURDO: *Oh* yes, Mr Hood.

CHARLEY: I'd like you to imagine what it's like to be old.

DONALD: What do you know about 'old'?

CHARLEY: I know.

DONALD: You're not old.

CHARLEY: I am old. Old and decrepit compared to young Murdo here. And I have to say old cunts like me get sensations young cunts know fuck all about, Murdo. Take knackered, take frustrated, take demoralised. Take *what the fuck you like*. So you're knackered, frustrated, demoralised and in for a work-out one night, you walk into Donald – the touch – Dick. Aye, you walk into him a state of imminent collapse, he offers you a large dod of *release*, you jump at it. (Fuck.) Don't you? Because what Donald offers *is* release. Release? It's not release: it's pure jobbying *therapy*. Other words, an antidote that bogging shitehole a city out there. And. So see this therapy, right? This therapy should take pride of place in any scheme make Glasgow a wholly healthy city. So, for fuck's sake, Murdo, you stroll into the massage chambers, one afternoon, by chance, it happens to the lot of us, you stroll into the massage chambers one afternoon half-way to a wholly healthy Glasgow recognize the apparently disgusting vision you see before you for what it really is; *therapy*.

DONALD: Is it fuck therapy. It's a pornophallic half-baked grope the dark, you don't know what hot wet object you'll put your hand on *next*.

CHARLEY: And. Pay no attention Donny's terminology. Pay no attention Donny's attitude. Because Donny's terminology, attitude is *up to him*. It's the *effect* of Donny's work in therapy concerns you me, Murdo. Us wholly healthy Glasgwegians.

MURDO: If this therapy has a role in the health of the body why wasn't it included in the ten-day initiation training-course?

DONALD: Exactly.

MURDO: So if this therapy were to be included in a wholly healthy Glasgow we'd have to ask Mr Bybugger's *permission* first. (Sorry.)

Pause.

CHARLEY: So. Asking Bobby Bybugger's permission? Aye ra ha ha now there's a problem. And. You feel you can *trust* Bobby Bybugger about therapy and a wholly healthy Glasgow do you?

MURDO: Oh, ah/

CHARLEY: Because answer me a question Murdo: Has Bybugger ever lied to you?

MURDO: Oh, ah/

CHARLEY: *Has* he?

MURDO: Yes. (Sorry.)

Pause.

CHARLEY: The sausage?

MURDO: Yes. The sausage.

CHARLEY: Well don't worry about Bobby lying *to you*. Because Bobby has also lied *to me*.

MURDO: Oh, what lie/?

CHARLEY: OK, I'm at Pontefract. Bybugger goes: 'You ya cunt. Dare renew anybody pre-sixth visit you're booted.' So I get back to Glasgow, I discover this talent I've got for enrolling, renewing in practically the same bastarding breath. So OK, I admit it: I totally ignore the six-visits rule. See any sign Bobby saying no to all the cash I bring him in.

MURDO: Is this true? . . . Mr Dick, is this true?

DONALD: Get to fuck, Murdo. You don't trust me.

CHARLEY: Thank fuck for which.

MURDO: Because I thought the six-visits rule was *essential* to give the member time to understand the value of the early-cheap-rate renewal.

CHARLEY: Is it fuck. The six-visits rule is because Bybugger assumes his staff are a load of untalented zombie ignoramuses like him that can't even make the members minds up for them. So, Murdo. Now you know the truth about Bybugger, here's the ultimate question your life. You going to fight for a wholly healthy Glasgow, alone if necessary, or piss about defeating yourself asking Bobby Bybugger's permission?

MURDO: Oh, ah/

CHARLEY: A wholly healthy Glasgow or a broken-backed wanker like Bobby Bybugger? Which?

MURDO: Does this mean I can't trust Mr Bybugger or, or *anybody*?

CHARLEY: Which?

MURDO: Oh, ah/

DONALD: Aye, *which*, for fuck's sake.

CHARLEY: Which.

Long pause.

MURDO: A wholly healthy Glasgow.

Pause.

CHARLEY: Congratulations.

DONALD: Off your nut. Biggest fuck up your that life decision.

CHARLEY: That's 'Donald' for 'A very impressive move there, Murdo son gorgeous.'

MURDO: Oh, ah but in what ways is Mr Bybugger a broken-backed wanker?

CHARLEY: Well, son. Say a punter begs him accept £200 cash, he goes: 'Sure you wouldn't like a *couple of years* think it over?'

DONALD: Aye. And he's a /

CHARLEY: Or. He takes on 50p-a-week punters that *don't come back*.

DONALD: And he's a/

CHARLEY: Or. He gives it away *free* he likes the sight their tit.

DONALD: And he's a useless fuck.

CHARLEY: Of course he is. Exactly. Who told you?

MURDO: Mr Bybugger is not a useless fuck.

CHARLEY: Who told you?

MURDO: Mr Bybugger is not a useless fuck, I said . . . Because/

CHARLEY: Donny: *who told you*?

DONALD: Alana told me.

CHARLEY: Who told Alana?

MURDO: Because I experimented sexually with Mr Bybugger.

Pause.

DONALD: I *thought* you were half bent.

MURDO: Are *you* tolerant of sexual experimentation, Mr Hood?

Pause.

DONALD: Very tolerant is our Charley. Aren't you son?

MURDO: And are *you* tolerant of sexual experimentation, Mr Dick?

DONALD: Get to fuck. I'm sorry, but I'm old-fashioned.

Pause.

CHARLEY: You miserable bastard you, Donald Dick.

DONALD: Don't you 'miserable bastard' me, Charley Hood. I've been *good* to you: I kept the Alana Bobby secret all these years. It takes a Murdo arrival before *that* comes out.

CHARLEY: (Years?)

Pause.

Murdo, son.

MURDO: Yes, Mr Hood.

CHARLEY: Do me a favour, uh? Go see you can see Craigie Stein the bar, the Empire Hotel, uh?

MURDO: I don't mind going for you, Mr Hood. But what if Mr Bybugger sees me?

CHARLEY: Don't go *right in* the bar. Stay *the doorway*. Take *a look*.

MURDO: And what if I do see Mr Stein?

CHARLEY: Just come back and tell me. Tell me he's alone, who he's with, *whatever*. (Fuck.)

CHARLEY *fumbles for cigarettes as* MURDO *goes to go*. CHARLEY *remembers*.

In fact: *fuck* . . . So Murdo: pick us up a packet of cigarettes, uh?

Pause.

MURDO: You don't smoke, Mr Hood.

MURDO *goes out to reception*.

Long pause.

DONALD: 'You don't smoke, Mr Hood.'

CHARLEY: Alana and Bobby?

DONALD: I don't think I'll *ever* like Murdo.

CHARLEY: Bobby and Alana?

DONALD: So, I'll maybe just go to London.

CHARLEY: Bobby and *Alana*?

DONALD: But when I think of the years I've spent accumulating these massage chambers: my shagpile, my atmosphere, my nooky.

CHARLEY: My Alana . . . Where *is* my Alana?

Pause.

DONALD: But I'll *have to* go to London *now*.

CHARLEY: You'll *have* to/? No you *won't* have to go to London.

DONALD: I do.

CHARLEY: Because I got Murdo brought round.

DONALD: Because I'll *never* get used to Murdo.

CHARLEY: But Murdo's *brought round* on your nooky, I says. (Fuck.)

DONALD: I'm going to London.

CHARLEY: Don't act it. You wouldn't go/ London? . . . *London*? I've *got* it, Donny boy son: I'll come to London *with* you.

DONALD: Fuck off.

CHARLEY: Because what does it *feel like* being a bastarding disgusting bender?

DONALD: Aye and you came to London with me the Earl's Court Road would empty in two seconds flat.

CHARLEY: Aye would it? Because *will I fuck* come to London with you. London? That shiting esoteric wankhole down south. And. Don't come it, Donny boy son. You're not going to London. Because London doesn't *give a fuck*. I mean: you're staggering home some Saturday night swearing your nut off you didn't get your nooky. What cunt's going to stop take time give you the bat the mouth you deserve? Uh? London? London: nooky every fifteen seconds? I pissed my pants. Aye London: who the fuck would *have* you?

DONALD: I had a fabulous life in London.

CHARLEY: London! It's a Glasgow guy a Lloret de Mar suntan you want. An international footballer a bad leg you're into. You don't get *them* London. All you get London's stockbrokers, artistic directors, Members of Parliament, perverts like that.

DONALD: Right now, I am so bastarding nooky-less, a Member of Parliament would do me fine.

CHARLEY: But if you had a *choice*, Donny. A choice between a Member of Parliament, his own TV show, and a broke-down fucked wreck a Glasgow footballer never washed his feet his life which would it be, uh? I mean: take your time consult you *conscience* on this.

DONALD: If a member of Parliament walked in here and the Member of Parliament was willing I'd have the Member of Parliament rotten. Because I want my nooky.

CHARLEY: OK. Because I want my renewal. My renewal? I want my Alana . . . Where is Alana?

DONALD: I don't know, Charley. But *if* she's with the footballer she's probably having a *fabulous* time.

CHARLEY: Oh Donny boy, son, don't/

DONALD: And if she *is* with him I suppose I might have to end up making do with her telling me *how* fabulous it was, afterwards.

CHARLEY: Oh don't say that, Donny.

DONALD: Things bad, uh?

CHARLEY: Donny, son.

DONALD: Because don't worry.

CHARLEY: Donny boy, son. Things are/

DONALD: Because the way things are going for you, Charley Hood, they'll get a lot worse *yet*.

Pause.

CHARLEY: Thanks.

DONALD: That's all right.

CHARLEY: Thanks, Donny.

DONALD: Don't mention it.

Pause.

I don't know how you can't just find yourself some other bird.

CHARLEY: I am not finding another bird.

DONALD: Because there's plenty them going about.

CHARLEY: Where else am I going to get a bird without an anti-climax? Because what other fucking bird you have to send a search party out for every other night?

Pause.

MURDO (*off, on tannoy*): Instructor to reception. Instructor to reception, please. Thank you.

Pause.

CHARLEY: Did some one speak?

MURDO (*off, on tannoy*): Instructor to reception please.

CHARLEY: Did I hear that?

MURDO (*off, on tannoy*): Instructor to reception, please. Thank you.

DONALD: You heard it.

CHARLEY: No way do I answer that.

DONALD: *Don't you dare* answer that.

CHARLEY: Because Murdo will have to/

MURDO (*off, on tannoy*): Charley Hood to/ Oh, ah will Charley Hood proceed directly to the gym please. The new member will be waiting for you there.

Pause.

CHARLEY: New member? *What* new member?

DONALD: What *next*?

Pause.

CHARLEY: Maybe, Donny, we should get Murdo to beat it, *after all*?

DONALD *turns slowly to* CHARLEY.

MURDO *comes in from reception, carrying the closed circuit monitor. He has two sheets of paper tucked into his track suit bottoms.*

He doesn't knock.

MURDO: Mr Bybugger has apologised for shouting at me.

DONALD: Look who's back. What kept you?

MURDO: He didn't need to.

DONALD: Been having your experimental nooky again?

MURDO: And Mr Bybugger thinks I'm a great guy with a great future.

CHARLEY: You weren't supposed to go *in* the bar, the Empire Hotel.

MURDO: Oh, but I did, Mr Hood. To pick up your cigarettes.

MURDO *produces and gives* CHARLEY *his cigarettes.* CHARLEY *takes them.* MURDO *sets up monitor during next speech.*

Didn't I? . . . Because I can tolerate *anything* now. I'm even going to tolerate you smoking on the way to a wholly healthy Glasgow. Mr Bybugger thinks a wholly healthy Glasgow is a wonderful publicity idea, by the way. So, you needn't worry about him. He's also very interested in your therapy, Donald. He's considering including it in the ten-day

initiation training-course. Which proves Mr Bybugger is a genuine human being. Doesn't it?

Pause.

CHARLEY: What's that?

CHARLEY *snatches one of the sheets from* MURDO.

Heh. This is a *renewal contract*. What the fuck's/?

MURDO: Oh, ah Mr Bybugger persuaded Mr Stein to renew.

CHARLEY: Mr Stein?

MURDO: Yes.

CHARLEY (*verifying it*): Craig Duff Stein. (Fuck.) Wait a minute. (*Looking elsewhere in the contract.*) It says: 'Signed by: Murdo Caldwell'.

MURDO: Yes. Mr Bybugger asked me to *finish off* his renewal.

CHARLEY: That was *my* renewal.

MURDO: Because Mr Bybugger wanted to finish off a *new* enrolment.

MURDO *produces the other sheet of paper.*

I sent him on down to the gym, for you.

CHARLEY *glances at it.*

And I *enjoyed* finishing off Mr Stein's renewal.

CHARLEY (*attending to new sheet*): Free? A free one? What's going on?

DONALD *settles down in front of closed circuit monitor.*

MURDO: Oh, ah Mr Bybugger is in a very *generous* mood.

CHARLEY: Generous with my livelihood.

DONALD: With my nooky.

MURDO: And a very happy mood.

CHARLEY: Happy? See you Murdo, you/

MURDO: And Mr Bybugger says I'm a very talented salesman. And that I *don't* have to stick to the gym department. Oh, yes. I can sell or do therapy, if I like.

CHARLEY: You Murdo are/

MURDO: And he said that you're quite right, Mr Hood. The six-visits rule *is* for untalented staff only.

CHARLEY: I have only one thing left to say to you.

MURDO: I've *never seen* Mr Bybugger in such a wonderful mood.

CHARLEY: Fuck you.

DONALD: Oh ho.

CHARLEY: And fuck you rigid.

DONALD: Ah huh.

MURDO: So he gave me the night off to prepare for my first big day tomorrow . . . Oh yes a much better mood. Because he said to me that sometimes Glasgow is a very surprising place, a very experimental place and then he winked at me as he got into the lift with Alana and Mr Stein. What did that mean, do you think?

Pause.

MURDO *goes to go.*

CHARLEY: So, Murdo.

MURDO *stops.*

MURDO: Yes?

CHARLEY: You're not really thinking of sticking around this back alley health joint?

MURDO: Oh, ah yes, Mr Hood.

CHARLEY: Because Spartan Health/

MURDO: Don't please, Mr Hood.

CHARLEY: Because Bobby Bybugger is a, a, a, a, rusting redundant vasectomy in a refrigerated dildo. A diabolical floating shite in a/

MURDO: Mr Hood. Don't waste your breath.

CHARLEY: In a/

MURDO: I *know* all that.

CHARLEY: In a/

MURDO: And I'm taking it in my stride because I'm so enthusiastic, so tolerant, so committed to a wholly healthy Glasgow.

DONALD: Would that kind of talk not just give you the vomit?

MURDO: And because you, because you *two* are so irrelevant.

MURDO *goes out to reception, repeating*

Irrelevant, irrelevant, irrelevant.

CHARLEY: So Donny boy, son. So what do you think is *wrong* this Murdo character? I mean: I tell him he's the brilliantist guy the world. I offer him one your free massages. I go: I'll help you out a wholly healthy Glasgow. Because you think some all that would stir up feelings of *obligation*, would you not? So therefore Donny: this Murdo character has no normal human feelings for me to take advantage of . . . *Has he?*

Pause.

DONALD: So, Charley.

CHARLEY: What, Donny?

DONALD: Get to fuck.

DONALD *adjusts close circuit.*

CHARLEY *takes out cigarette, lights it and takes a puff.*

CHARLEY: So what you looking at?

DONALD: Nothing.

Pause.

But get that cigarette out.

CHARLEY *takes a puff.*

Because I've got my shagpile to think about.

CHARLEY: Oh see your shagpile:/

DONALD: I'm occupied.

CHARLEY *looks at his cigarette thoughtfully.* DONALD *adjusts closed circuit.*

But get that cigarette/

CHARLEY: OK, Donny. I will.

CHARLEY *stubs the cigarette out systematically into the shagpile.* DONALD *watches horrified until he is distracted by the closed circuit.*

DONALD: Who's that? . . Who's that the gym?

CHARLEY *goes to look.*

I think that's the/

CHARLEY: I don't know.

DONALD: Oh, God help me. It's the porter, the Empire Hotel.

Pause.

CHARLEY: Aye ra ha ha, you kill me. So after I renew this porter guy, do you want me to line you him up?

DONALD: Get to fuck . . . I might have a line up of my own.

CHARLEY: OK.

DONALD: I might have a line up of my own, *I said.*

CHARLEY: *OK.* (And that *will be* right.)

DONALD: That *is* right. A line up/ A *therapy* of my own.

CHARLEY: A therapy?

DONALD: I'm occupied.

Pause.

CHARLEY: So tomorrow, Donny: *new plans.*

DONALD: Get to hell.

CHARLEY: New plans to get rid the new boy.

DONALD: Because I'm all right as I am.

CHARLEY: The new instructor. (Fuck.)

DONALD: I'm occupied.

CHARLEY: Tomorrow!

CHARLEY goes towards gym exit as lights fade.